Google JAX Essentials

A quick practical learning of blazing-fast library for machine learning and deep learning projects

Mei Wong

Copyright © 2023 by GitforGits.

Published by: GitforGits
Publisher: Sonal Dhandre
www.gitforgits.com
support@gitforgits.com

Printed in India

First Printing: May 2023

ISBN: 978-8196288358

Cover Design by: Kitten Publishing

For permission to use material from this book, please contact GitforGits at support@gitforgits.com.

Content

Preface

"Google JAX Essentials" is a comprehensive guide designed for machine learning and deep learning professionals aiming to leverage the power and capabilities of Google's JAX library in their projects. Over the course of eight chapters, this book takes the reader from understanding the challenges of deep learning and numerical computations in the existing frameworks to the essentials of Google JAX, its functionalities, and how to leverage it in real-world machine learning and deep learning projects.

The book starts by emphasizing the importance of numerical computing in ML and DL, demonstrating the limitations of traditional libraries like NumPy, and introducing the solution offered by JAX. It then guides the reader through the installation of JAX on different computing environments like CPUs, GPUs, and TPUs, and its integration into existing ML and DL projects. Moving further, the book details the advanced numerical operations and unique features of JAX, including JIT compilation, automatic differentiation, batched operations, and custom gradients. It illustrates how these features can be employed to write code that is both simpler and faster. The book also delves into parallel computation, the effective use of the vmap function, and the use of pmap for distributed computing.

Lastly, the reader is walked through the practical application of JAX in training different deep learning models, including RNNs, CNNs, and Bayesian models, with additional focus on performance tuning strategies for JAX applications.

In this book you will learn how to:

- Mastering the installation and configuration of JAX on various computing environments.
- Understanding the intricacies of JAX's advanced numerical operations.
- Harnessing the power of JIT compilation in JAX for accelerated computations.
- Implementing batched operations using the vmap function for efficient processing.
- Leveraging automatic differentiation and custom gradients in JAX.
- Proficiency in using the pmap function for distributed computing in JAX.
- Training different types of deep learning models using JAX.
- Applying performance tuning strategies to maximize JAX application efficiency.
- Integrating JAX into existing machine learning and deep learning projects.
- Complementing the official JAX documentation with practical, real-world applications.

This book is an enhanced practical guide that complements the official JAX documentation. Written by subject experts in JAX and Deep Learning, it is aimed at enabling readers to become proficient and hands-on with JAX for their ML and DL projects.

GitforGits

Prerequisites

This is must read for machine learning and deep learning professionals to be skilled with the most innovative deep learning library. Knowing Python and experience with machine learning is sufficient to begin with this book

Codes Usage

Are you in need of some helpful code examples to assist you in your programming and documentation? Look no further! Our book offers a wealth of supplemental material, including code examples and exercises.

Not only is this book here to aid you in getting your job done, but you have our permission to use the example code in your programs and documentation. However, please note that if you are reproducing a significant portion of the code, we do require you to contact us for permission.

But don't worry, using several chunks of code from this book in your program or answering a question by citing our book and quoting example code does not require permission. But if you do choose to give credit, an attribution typically includes the title, author, publisher, and ISBN. For example, "Google JAX Essentials by Mei Wong".

If you are unsure whether your intended use of the code examples falls under fair use or the permissions outlined above, please do not hesitate to reach out to us at support@gitforgits.com.

We are happy to assist and clarify any concerns.

Acknowledgement

I owe a tremendous debt of gratitude to GitforGits, for their unflagging enthusiasm and wise counsel throughout the entire process of writing this book. Their knowledge and careful editing helped make sure the piece was useful for people of all reading levels and comprehension skills. In addition, I'd like to thank everyone involved in the publishing process for their efforts in making this book a reality. Their efforts, from copyediting to advertising, made the project what it is today.

Finally, I'd like to express my gratitude to everyone who has shown me unconditional love and encouragement throughout my life. Their support was crucial to the completion of this book. I appreciate your help with this endeavour and your continued interest in my career.

Prologue

Welcome to this comprehensive guide on Google's JAX, a powerful library for numerical computation that has been making waves in the machine learning and deep learning communities. This book aims to arm you with the knowledge and hands-on skills to harness the full potential of JAX in your projects and experiments.

The field of machine learning and deep learning is ever-evolving, with new tools, libraries, and techniques being introduced frequently. One such transformative introduction has been Google's JAX. With its unique features, such as JIT compilation, automatic differentiation, vectorization, and parallel computing capabilities, JAX fills many gaps left by traditional Python libraries like NumPy.

This book is structured in a way that takes you from understanding the need for JAX, its development and evolution, to getting hands-on with the library, and finally leveraging its powerful features in real-world scenarios. We'll start by addressing the challenges in numerical computing and how JAX can be the answer to many of those challenges.

We will then dive into JAX's installation process across different environments and understand how to integrate it into your existing machine learning projects. In the middle chapters, we'll focus on understanding and utilizing the advanced numerical operations capabilities of JAX. From efficient indexing and JIT compilation to batch operations, automatic differentiation, and handling of control flow statements, you'll learn to appreciate the flexibility and power JAX offers.

Further, the book goes in-depth into using JAX for parallel computing and batch processing, which are integral components of deep learning. We'll learn how to use JAX's unique 'pmap' and 'vmap' functions to speed up computations and improve performance.

Towards the end of the book, we will be applying our understanding of JAX to real-world machine learning and deep learning projects. This section will guide you through using JAX to train models like CNNs, RNNs, and Bayesian models, demonstrating how JAX can be an instrumental tool in the deep learning landscape.

This book, while extensive and thorough, is not meant to replace the official JAX documentation. Instead, consider it as a comprehensive companion and practical guide, enhancing the material provided in the official documentation with additional insights, practical examples, and real-world applications.

Whether you are a machine learning enthusiast, a professional researcher, or a deep learning practitioner, this book will equip you with the necessary knowledge and skills to use JAX effectively. So, let's get started on this exciting journey of exploring and mastering Google's JAX. Here's to our journey towards creating more efficient and powerful machine learning and deep learning models!

CHAPTER 1: NECESSITY FOR GOOGLE JAX

The era of the data explosion has brought about the advent of Machine Learning (ML) and Deep Learning (DL), both of which are strong computational tools that are able to learn from large volumes of data and make intelligent predictions and judgments. The significance of numerical computing is becoming more and more obvious as these fields continue to advance.

Importance of Numerical Computing in Deep Learning

Machine learning and deep learning both rely heavily on computational mathematics in order to function properly. It encapsulates the mathematical processes that fuel anything from the simplest linear regression model to the most sophisticated neural network. It is the backbone that enables machines to learn from data. The application of mathematical procedures to numerical data is the focus of the field of computing known as numerical computing. Calculus (containing derivatives, gradients, and optimization), statistics (including probability distribution and random number generation), linear algebra (including vectors, matrices, and tensor operations), and more are all a part of it. It is utilized for the manipulation and study of numbers. These are the fundamental elements that make up machine learning and deep learning algorithms.

For example, Deep Learning employs multilayer neural networks, where each layer does complex numerical computations. This type of learning is known as "deep learning." The term "deep learning" refers to the presence of numerous layers within the neural network. Imagine that each of these levels has millions of neurons, and that each neuron is responsible for completing computations and passing the results on to the next layer; the sheer volume of numerical operations is mind-boggling.

In order to train these models, we employ optimization strategies such as gradient descent, which allow us to iteratively tune the model parameters and, as a result, reduce the amount of inaccuracy in the predictions. Every iteration requires computing gradients, which is a procedure that requires a substantial amount of numerical operations. Therefore, having capabilities for effective numerical calculation is of the utmost importance to assure the practicability and swiftness of the training of these models.

Numerical Computing Challenges in ML and DL

For all intents and purposes, carrying out numerical computations on a massive scale is not an easy undertaking. These procedures frequently call for a high level of precision, and because even very insignificant numerical errors have the potential to compound over time, the results may end up being significantly off target. In addition, a large number of numerical computations are highly parallelizable. This means that they can be segmented into more manageable jobs that can be carried out in parallel with one another. This is especially true for many of the matrix operations that are used in machine learning and deep learning. These operations can be computed much more quickly if we can harness the parallel computation capabilities of modern hardware such as GPUs and TPUs. This is especially true for many of the matrix operations that are used in machine learning and deep learning.

Traditional numerical computing libraries, such as NumPy, do not, however, meet all of these requirements, hence they are not suitable. NumPy is a terrific tool that has been of service to the Python community for years, but when it was first developed, it was not intended with parallel processing or hardware accelerators in mind. As a direct consequence of this, it does not natively support operations on GPUs or TPUs, which are becoming an increasingly vital component of high-performance machine learning and deep learning.

This is when the JAX library from Google comes into play. JAX is an extension to NumPy that was designed to keep the simplicity and ease-of-use of the NumPy interface while offering extra features that are specifically tuned for high-performance numerical computations. JAX was developed as an open-source project. Python programmers are able to take advantage of the full capability of modern hardware thanks to this feature, which provides automatic differentiation, vectorization, parallelization, and just-in-time (JIT) compilation to machine code.

To summarize, numerical computing is an essential component of machine learning and deep learning because it manages the complex mathematical operations that are necessary for automated systems to acquire knowledge from data. The necessity for high-performance numerical computing libraries that are able to fully use the capabilities of modern hardware has never been more obvious than it is now, due to the growing complexity and scope of modern machine learning and deep learning models. New tools like JAX, which aim to overcome these limits and drive the next generation of machine learning research, can be better appreciated if we first grasp the challenges given by large-scale numerical calculations in machine learning and deep learning.

Case Studies: Where Traditional Approaches Struggle

Let us have a look at three exemplary examples using Deep Learning (DL) projects in order to get a better understanding of the obstacles and limitations posed by standard numerical computing methodologies.

Case Study 1: Training Large-Scale Language Models

The introduction of transformer-based models such as GPT-4, BERT, and RoBERTa has resulted in important developments in the field of Natural Language Processing (NLP). These models can have hundreds of millions of parameters, or even billions, and require considerable training on massive text corpora. The numerical computations that are required for training these models are both large and sophisticated in nature.

For instance, matrix multiplications and computations of activation functions for each layer of the model are required in both the forward and backward runs of the training process. The sheer scale of these computations is mind-boggling when one considers the breadth and depth of these models. In addition, gradient calculations are necessary for the parameter updates that are part of the optimization process, which frequently includes variations on stochastic gradient descent.

Training such huge models with conventional tools like NumPy or even specialized machine learning frameworks can be a difficult task due to the complexity of the data. It is possible for the training process to move at an excruciatingly snail's pace if there is no way to efficiently employ contemporary hardware accelerators like GPUs or TPUs for parallel computations. Because of this inability to fully use the capability of parallel processing units, computational bottlenecks can occur, which can extend the time it takes to complete a project and may restrict the size and complexity of models that can be properly trained.

Case Study 2: Large Scale Image Analysis and Object Detection

Another domain where DL has had a revolutionary impact is computer vision. Complex models such as Convolutional Neural Networks (CNNs) and their derivatives are utilized for a variety of tasks, including image classification, object recognition, and semantic segmentation, etc.

Take for example a project that entails teaching a model to recognize and categorize different types of items contained within high-resolution photographs. The model needs to search through potentially millions of pixels in each image in order to recognize recurring patterns and distinguishing features. At every level, including the initial preprocessing and normalization of picture input, the convolutional layers where filters are applied, and the final stages where bounding boxes are predicted, numerical operations are performed. Again, the scale of the computations involved can be rather large, particularly when working with photos or video data that have a high resolution.

When working with such large-scale image data, the limitations of typical numerical computing packages become readily evident. It is possible that the speed and efficiency of model training and inference will suffer dramatically if there is no way to effectively divide these computations over several processing units.

Case Study 3: Complex Reinforcement Learning Environments

Training an agent to make decisions that are optimal within a particular environment is the goal of the reinforcement learning (RL) technique. Some RL projects take place in extremely intricate and multi-dimensional settings. Take, for example, the case of teaching an agent how to play a video game, where the state space encompasses each and every conceivable permutation of the game's variables.

Training a deep neural network to estimate the ideal action-value function is one of the steps involved in running the popular Deep Q-Network (DQN) algorithm in RL. Each update in DQN comprises a series of numerous stages of numerical computations. These steps include forward passes to calculate current estimates and goal Q-values, as well as backward passes to compute gradients and update the weights. The state and action spaces in large-scale RL systems can be exceedingly massive, which results in a significant number of numerical computations required for each update. The computational burden may be difficult for traditional tools to handle, which may result in long training times and impede the agent's ability to properly learn the best strategy.

These case studies illustrate the difficulties that can arise when attempting to scale numerical computations for deep learning projects by use more conventional methods. Even though libraries such as NumPy have been of great use to us for a number of years, their capacity to deal with the volume and complexity of modern machine learning is severely lacking. They do not provide support for operations on contemporary hardware accelerators, which may result in significant inefficiencies and processing bottlenecks. This is one of the reasons why the creation of new tools like Google's JAX is so intriguing. JAX is able to assist in overcoming the restrictions that are inherent to standard numerical computing libraries since it provides automatic differentiation, vectorization, parallelization, and just-in-time compilation. It paves the way for ever more daring efforts in machine learning and deep learning and enables us to take on issues that are both larger and more complicated than ever before.

Summary

In the midst of the period of the data explosion, we have witnessed the rise of Machine Learning (ML) and Deep Learning (DL), both of which are enabled by the fundamental basis of numerical computing. Computing on a numerical scale is the fulcrum that supports the extensive and sophisticated mathematical operations that allow these models to learn from data and generate predictions based on that learning. However, the growing complexity and scale of modern ML and DL models has highlighted the necessity for high-performance numerical computing libraries. This is especially important when taking into consideration the large-scale computations that are required as well as the possibility of mistake accumulation.

Traditional numerical computing tools, such as NumPy, create hurdles when applied to modern-day machine learning and deep learning endeavors, despite the fact that they have served the Python community excellently for a number of years. When attempting to fully harness the potential of contemporary hardware accelerators for parallel computations, the limits of NumPy become increasingly evident. Because DL projects are getting bigger and the datasets are getting bigger, there is a greater demand for computation that is both efficient and quick. Examples like the training of large-scale language models, high-resolution image analysis and object detection, and complicated reinforcement learning environments bring to light the deficiencies of traditional tools in terms of numerical calculation, efficiency, and speed. These examples demonstrate the drawbacks of traditional tools in a clear and concise manner.

At this point, Google's JAX comes into its own as a viable option. JAX is an extension of NumPy that keeps the straightforward nature of the NumPy interface while providing essential functions specifically geared toward high-performance numerical calculation. JAX enables Python developers to fully leverage the potential of modern hardware by providing automatic differentiation, vectorization, parallelization, and just-in-time (JIT) compilation. This, in turn, encourages the creation of increasingly complex ML and DL models. Understanding these issues and the subsequent development of tools such as JAX provides us with vital insights into the development of machine learning and deep learning as a whole, as well as the trajectory of their future.

Chapter 2:
Unraveling JAX

The Evolution of JAX at Google

An open-source library for numerical computing, JAX is an acronym that stands for "JIT, Autograd, and XLA." It was developed by Google. It was developed as an improved expansion of NumPy, which is a mainstay in the world of numerical computing and data analysis. It brought to the table additional features that were becoming increasingly important in the age of modern machine learning and deep learning.

Machine learning and artificial intelligence are two areas in which Google has been at the forefront of numerous pioneering developments in recent years. Google had a strong reason to develop tools that could help push the boundaries of what was feasible because it has products such as Google Search, Google Photos, and Google Translate, all of which rely significantly on machine learning models. Google's pursuit of improved efficiency and flexibility in numerical computing for machine learning served as the impetus for the development of the JAX programming language. Around the year 2015, researchers at Google began investigating ways in which they could make Python, a programming language that is admired by many for its ease of use and readability, quicker and more effective for doing the large-scale computations required by their complicated machine learning models.

One of the earliest results of these efforts was the creation of a Python package called Autograd by Dougal Maclaurin, David Duvenaud, and Matt Johnson. This package has the ability to automatically discriminate between code written in native Python and NumPy. It presented a method for calculating gradients, which are necessary for the training of deep learning models, using only Python as the language of operation. Autograd was a huge step forward, but it did not completely overcome the performance concerns that were connected with Python and NumPy. Around the same time, Google also published XLA, which stands for Accelerated Linear Algebra and is a domain-specific linear algebra compiler with the ability to optimize TensorFlow computations. It was developed to enhance the performance of TensorFlow operations; nevertheless, its potential was regarded as having far wider use. XLA provided a method for the generation of high-performance code for GPUs and TPUs, which is essential for doing large-scale machine learning computations.

Engineers at Google, including those who worked on Autograd, embarked on the creation of JAX, building on the foundations set by Autograd and XLA. JAX is an acronym that stands for Java Application Expressions. They envisioned a program that, similar to Autograd, would be able to automatically differentiate between students, but would also harness the potential of XLA to achieve higher levels of performance. In addition, they desired to provide users with the capacity to write their numerical computations in uncomplicated Python code, which would subsequently be just-in-time compiled into high-performance machine code. The result of this idea was the creation of JAX, which combines the advantages of Autograd and XLA while preserving the accessibility and ease of use of Python and NumPy. It was the first program to implement useful capabilities such as just-in-time (JIT) compilation of machine code, automatic differentiation, vectorization, and parallel processing. Google provided the research community with JAX, a tool that had the potential to make Python appropriate for high-performance machine learning and that had the ability to keep up with the increasing demands of modern machine learning workloads.

Today, academics and engineers all over the world are using JAX, which is helping to push the boundaries of what is possible in the fields of machine learning and artificial intelligence. Because it allows Python developers to fully exploit new hardware accelerators and applies advanced techniques like as automated differentiation and parallel computing, JAX has become a vital participant in the ever-evolving field of numerical computing for machine learning. This is because JAX provides an avenue for Python developers to fully leverage modern hardware accelerators. The quest at Google for increased efficiency and flexibility in numerical computation for machine learning has been the primary impetus for the development of JAX during the course of the company's history. JAX is a breakthrough in the field of machine learning that, by expanding on the achievements of Autograd and XLA, has made it possible for researchers and engineers to develop models that are both more complicated and more powerful than ever before.

Understanding JIT Compilation in JAX

Just-in-time (JIT) compilation is a robust capability that comes standard with JAX and is an essential component of the higher performance possibilities it offers. Every single operation in traditional Python is re-examined and re-interpreted at runtime. When you write a function in Python, the operations that you include in the function won't be turned into machine code until the very moment when the function is called and put into action. The execution of the code might be slowed down as a result of this, which is especially problematic in numerical computing, where we frequently have to repeat the same operations.

We are able to get around this overhead by utilizing the JIT compilation functionality that is available in JAX. Instead of interpreting operations while the program is running, JIT compiles the operations into efficient machine code before executing the program. The phrase "just-in-time" refers to the singular occurrence of this procedure, which occurs when the function is invoked for the very first time. After the code has been compiled, it is cached so that it can be used again in following calls; this results in significant speedups, particularly for more extensive computations.

Let us look at an example to better understand this. Suppose we have a function that is capable of doing matrix multiplication, which is a typical operation in machine learning.

```
import jax.numpy as jnp
from jax import jit

def matmul(x, y):
  return jnp.dot(x, y)

x = jnp.ones((5000, 5000))
y = jnp.ones((5000, 5000))

# Without JIT
%timeit matmul(x, y).block_until_ready()

# With JIT
jit_matmul = jit(matmul)
%timeit jit_matmul(x, y).block_until_ready()
```

In this demonstration, the matmul function is defined to multiply two matrices together. We measure the amount of time required to complete this function both with and without JIT. You will note that the JIT-compiled version of the function (jit_matmul) executes a lot quicker than the traditional version. This speedup is made possible by JIT compilation of the function into machine code that can be efficiently run on the hardware being targeted (such as a GPU or TPU). It is important to keep in mind, however, that JIT compilation does result in some additional overhead at the initial call to the function because the code needs to be compiled. However, for functions that are called multiple times, the speedups that occur during future calls typically more than compensate for the initial overhead that occurs on the first call.

The JIT feature of JAX is consequently a great tool for boosting the efficiency of numerical computations. It shines particularly brightly when working with huge arrays or complex operations that are repeated a significant number of times. Because JIT is able to convert Python code into machine code that is more efficient, we are able to utilize the full potential of contemporary hardware. This makes JAX a reliable option for high-performance machine learning workloads.

Understanding Auto-Differentiation in JAX

Auto-differentiation is yet another essential component of JAX, and it is an aspect that is absolutely necessary for the field of machine learning. In the fields of machine learning and particularly deep learning, the process of training a model frequently involves optimization methods like gradient descent, which require the computation of derivatives or gradients. This is particularly true in deep learning. Manually calculating these gradients can be a time-consuming and potentially error-prone process, particularly for complicated models with a large number of parameters.

By automating the process of computing derivatives, auto-differentiation provides a solution to this difficulty. It not only makes the task easier to complete, but it also improves its effectiveness and precision. Auto-differentiation is a method that provides a method to compute derivatives that strikes a balance between computational efficiency and numerical stability. This is in contrast to numerical differentiation, which can suffer from numerical instability, and symbolic differentiation, which can result in exponential growth in the requirements for computing. Users are able to compute the gradients of Python functions with very little effort thanks to the auto-differentiation feature of JAX, which is implemented through the grad function. It accomplishes this by employing the chain rule of calculus to simplify complex derivatives into simpler ones, thus changing the computation into a directed acyclic graph, and then evaluating this graph in an effective manner.

Let us look at an example to illustrate this. Suppose we have a simple function f(x) = x^2 + 3x + 1, and we want to find its derivative at x=2.

```
from jax import grad
import jax.numpy as jnp

def f(x):
    return x**2 + 3*x + 1

df = grad(f)

print(df(2.0))  # Prints "7.0"
```

In the above sample program, we define the function f and use JAX's grad function to create a new function df that computes the gradient of f. Evaluating df(2.0) gives us the value of the derivative of f at x=2.0, which is 7.0. This is equivalent to manually computing the derivative of f(x), which is 2x + 3, and evaluating it at x=2.0.

The auto-differentiation feature of JAX simplifies the process of computing gradients, making it a key asset in the training of machine learning models. It allows us to focus on designing our models and algorithms, leaving the intricate work of derivative computation to JAX.

Understanding XLA in JAX

The XLA compiler is the third fundamental component that makes up JAX. XLA, which is an abbreviation that stands for "Accelerated Linear Algebra," is a domain-specific compiler that was developed specifically for linear algebra computations. It is essential to the performance of JAX.

Vectorization and parallelization are two of the most important skills that XLA offers.

Vectorization is the act of transforming an algorithm from operating on a single value at a time to operating on a collection of values (a vector) at one time. This allows the algorithm to more efficiently analyze large amounts of data. Since central processing units (CPUs), graphics processing units (GPUs), and tensor processing units (TPUs) of modern computers are able to carry out operations simultaneously on whole vectors, vectorized operations are typically substantially faster than their non-vectorized equivalents.

On the other hand, completing many processes at the same time is what is meant by the term "parallelization." When referring to the field of machine learning, this typically refers to the practice of carrying out calculations on several components of a massive dataset in parallel. When working with enormous datasets or sophisticated models that cannot be processed sequentially in an efficient manner, parallel computing becomes an absolutely necessary tool.

This is made possible by XLA, which compiles Python code into an intermediate representation called HLO (High Level Optimizer). This representation can then be optimized for effective execution on hardware accelerators. This enables high-performance hardware like GPUs and TPUs to run your Python code without requiring you to write any specialized low-level code. This frees you from the burden of having to develop such code.

Let us look at an example to better understand these topics. Let us consider we have a huge array that we want to apply a function to in an element-by-element fashion.

```
import jax.numpy as jnp
from jax import vmap, jit

# Define a function
def func(x):
    return jnp.sin(x) ** 2

# Create a large array
x = jnp.linspace(0, 10, 1000000)

# Without vmap
output = jnp.array([func(xi) for xi in x])

# With vmap
vectorized_func = vmap(func)
output = vectorized_func(x)

# With vmap and JIT
vectorized_func = jit(vmap(func))
output = vectorized_func(x)
```

In the above sample program, we first apply func to x in a standard Python loop. This is slow and doesn't leverage the potential of modern hardware. Next, we use vmap to vectorize func, creating a new function vectorized_func that can be applied to an array of inputs at once. This is faster as it allows the computation to be performed on entire chunks of the array simultaneously.

Finally, we further optimize the computation by using JIT on top of vmap. This compiles the function into machine code using XLA, leading to even better performance.

Understanding Device Arrays in JAX

In JAX, computations can be run on a variety of hardware devices, including central processing units (CPUs), graphics processing units (GPUs), and tensor processing units (TPUs). In order to facilitate the management of the data stored on these devices, JAX introduces a notion that is known as "device arrays."

A device array in JAX is analogous to a NumPy array, with the key difference being that it resides on an accelerator device as opposed to the memory of the host (CPU). Whenever you perform operations on device arrays, such activities are carried out on the device that is now housing the array. It is because of this that you are able to make full use of the computing resources that modern hardware accelerators provide, and the high-performance capabilities that JAX possesses are in large part due to this feature.

Device arrays are immutable, much like NumPy arrays, which is something that you should keep in mind because it's vital. That means a device array, once it has been created, cannot have any changes made to it. Any operation that gives the impression that it is modifying a device array will, in reality, generate a brand new array.

Either by performing operations on already-existing device arrays or by moving data from a host to a device, it is possible to generate a new device array. Once you have a device array, every JAX action that you do on it will automatically run on the device where the array resides; explicit instructions are not required in this case.

Below is an example:

```
import jax.numpy as jnp
from jax import device_put

# Create a numpy array
x_np = np.array([1, 2, 3])

# Transfer array to device
x_device = device_put(x_np)

# x_device is now a device array
print(type(x_device))  # <class 'jaxlib.xla_extension.DeviceArray'>

# Perform operation on device array
y_device = jnp.sin(x_device)

# y_device is also a device array, and the computation was performed on the
```

device
```
print(type(y_device))  # <class 'jaxlib.xla_extension.DeviceArray'>
```

In the above sample program, we first create a NumPy array x_np. We then use the device_put function to transfer this array to a device, resulting in a device array x_device. When we apply the jnp.sin function to x_device, the operation is performed on the device, and the result y_device is also a device array.

Using Device Arrays in Machine Learning

When it comes to machine learning, device arrays appear to be even more effective than they were before. For instance, the parameters and gradients of a model can be represented as device arrays when the model is being trained. During each phase of the training process, tasks such as computing the gradient and updating the parameters can be carried out directly on these device arrays. This eliminates the necessity of exchanging data between the host and the device, resulting in training that is both more effective and more quickly accomplished.

Additionally, because JAX takes a functional approach, there is no need for you to be concerned about making in-place updates to device arrays. When using an eager execution framework like PyTorch, it is usual practice to make in-place updates to device tensors. This can create challenges for the process of developing code that is capable of being automatically differentiated or parallelized. These kinds of issues do not crop up in JAX since the device arrays are immutable and every action has a high level of functional purity.

In the context of machine learning, the following is an illustration of one possible application for device arrays:

```
from jax import grad, jit
from jax import random
import jax.numpy as jnp

# Create a simple linear regression model
def model(params, x):
    return jnp.dot(params, x)


# Define a loss function
```

```
def loss(params, x, y):
    y_pred = model(params, x)
    return jnp.mean((y_pred - y) ** 2)

# Compute gradients of the loss function
grad_loss = jit(grad(loss))

# Initialize parameters
params = random.normal(random.PRNGKey(0), (100,))

# Suppose we have some data
x = random.normal(random.PRNGKey(1), (100,))
y = random.normal(random.PRNGKey(2), (100,))

# Compute the gradient of the loss with respect to the parameters
grad_params = grad_loss(params, x, y)
```

In this particular illustration, the model's parameter arrays, the data, and the computed gradient arrays are all device arrays. The device is responsible for carrying out all computations, including the forward pass in the model, the loss computation, and the gradient computation. You are able to build code for numerical computations and machine learning that is both efficient and high-performing with the help of JAX's device arrays, which are a powerful feature of the language. They make it possible for you to make seamless use of current hardware accelerators, which ultimately results in the execution of your applications happening more quickly and effectively.

Understanding Pseudo-Random Number Generation in JAX

The generation of random numbers is dependent on hidden global state in both the classic Python programming environment and in many other contexts as well. Because these libraries keep an internal state that is changed with every call, this could be rather troublesome in a functionally pure context like JAX. In the context of parallel computing, it is difficult to provide guarantees regarding the order in which operations will take place. As a consequence, the order in which random number generation will take place is subject to uncertainty, which may result in outcomes that are impossible to reproduce.

On the other hand, the jax.random module of JAX implements a stateless, also known as "counter-based," pseudo-random number generator (PRNG). The pseudo-random number generator (PRNG) in JAX accepts a "key" as an explicit input and then delivers a random result along with a new key rather than keeping a mutable state that is updated with each new random number that is created.

It is possible to use jax.random to produce the first key, which is also referred to as a seed.PRNGKey(). When you have a key, you can use the functions in jax.random to produce random integers. Some of these functions are uniform(), normal(), and others. It is vitally important that each random operation make use of a different key. You can create a new key that is completely unique by utilizing the split() method, which takes a key as an argument and returns multiple new keys.

Below is one of the sample demonstration:

```
from jax import random

# Generate a key
key = random.PRNGKey(0)

# Split the key
key1, key2 = random.split(key, 2)

# Use the split keys to generate random numbers
rand1 = random.normal(key1)
rand2 = random.normal(key2)


print(rand1, rand2)  # Should print two different random numbers
```

In this demonstration, we begin by generating a key with the PRNGKey() function. After that, we use the split() function to create two new keys from this key, and then we utilize these keys to generate two random integers. The random numbers that we created are distinct from one another since we employed a variety of keys.

The creation of random numbers using this method has a number of advantages. It provides you with complete control over the random state, which can be of great use when testing and debugging software. Given the same keys, it also guarantees that random operations are deterministic and reproducible in the system. Because there is no hidden state, this method is compatible with the functional programming style of JAX, as well as its JIT compilation and parallelization features.

Summary

We looked at the key aspects of Google's JAX library that make it an efficient and powerful tool for numerical computing in machine learning and deep learning in this chapter. Just-in-time (JIT) compilation, auto-differentiation, accelerated linear algebra (XLA), device arrays, and a novel method to pseudo-random number generation are among the features.

The first notable feature, JIT compilation, enables Python functions to be turned into efficient machine code prior to execution, resulting in significant speed increases in computations. This is especially useful for routines that include loops or are called several times. Another key feature is auto-differentiation, which automates the computation of derivatives and gradients, making it easier to implement many machine learning methods. The grad function, which can generate gradients for arbitrary Python functions, is responsible for JAX's auto-differentiation.

XLA extends the power of JAX by providing vectorization and parallel computation, optimizing your Python code for fast execution on high-performance hardware such as GPUs and TPUs. Device arrays handle data on these devices, allowing computations to be performed where the data exists, reducing data transfers and increasing performance. Device arrays are generated by performing operations on existing device arrays or by moving data from the host to a device. Any JAX operation done on it after it is created will be performed on the device where the array is stored. Finally, we looked at JAX's solution to pseudo-random number generation, which keeps functional purity by being stateless and counter-based, making random number generation predictable and reproducible given the same keys.

In essence, JAX improves NumPy's capabilities by providing a set of sophisticated features, transforming Python into a high-performance numerical computing language. Its unique approach to JIT compilation, auto-differentiation, the power of XLA, and the utilization of device arrays, together with its new approach to pseudo-random number generation, make JAX a useful tool in the toolkit of any machine learning researcher or practitioner.

CHAPTER 3: SETTING UP JAX FOR MACHINE LEARNING AND DEEP LEARNING

JAX Prerequisites

JAX, a library for high-performance machine learning research, can operate on various kinds of hardware platforms including CPUs, GPUs, and TPUs. Prior to embarking on the installation process, understanding the requirements for each type of hardware is crucial.

Starting with CPUs, JAX functions seamlessly on any system capable of running Python and NumPy. Python, a general-purpose programming language, and NumPy, a Python library used for numerical computations, form the base requirement for JAX. For optimal performance, it is advised to use a modern version of Python (3.7 or above) along with the latest release of NumPy. This combination ensures the efficient execution of JAX on the CPU.

Moving onto GPUs, JAX compatibility extends to systems possessing a CUDA-enabled GPU with a corresponding version of the CUDA SDK. CUDA (Compute Unified Device Architecture) is a parallel computing platform developed by NVIDIA, enabling drastic increases in computing performance by harnessing the power of the graphics processing unit. JAX, as of the latest update, was congruent with CUDA 10.1 or above and cuDNN 7.6 or above. cuDNN is a GPU-accelerated library for deep neural networks that allows JAX to leverage the computational power of GPUs. In case the CUDA SDK is not installed, it can be downloaded from the NVIDIA official website. It is also important to install cuDNN for deep learning computations. The compatibility of your CUDA and cuDNN versions with your JAX version is a critical consideration when preparing for JAX installation on GPUs.

Lastly, regarding TPUs or Tensor Processing Units, the process is slightly more complex. TPUs are specialized hardware accelerators engineered by Google and are accessible exclusively via Google Cloud. For JAX to function on TPUs, a Google Cloud project with TPU access needs to be set up. Subsequently, JAX code execution takes place on a VM within that specific project. The installation of libtpu and tensorflow packages is also mandatory. They provide the essential software structure for TPU usage. Always ensure to choose versions of these packages that synchronize with your JAX version.

Bear in mind that JAX's installation process will differ based on the target hardware. The CPU version of JAX cannot operate with GPUs or TPUs, and similarly, the GPU version is incompatible with TPUs. Therefore, defining the hardware you aim to use prior to beginning the installation process is of paramount importance.

In the upcoming sections, we delve into the detailed procedure of installing JAX for each distinct type of hardware, ensuring a comprehensive understanding of the process and requirements. This serves as a critical learning for optimizing JAX's potential across various hardware configurations, thereby driving more efficient and powerful machine learning research.

Installing JAX on CPU

Installing JAX on a CPU (for a Linux system) is quite straightforward, as it can be installed via pip, the Python package installer. Firstly, it's a good practice to create a virtual environment for your project. This helps to keep your project and its dependencies self-contained, and it can prevent conflicts between packages required by different projects.

Below is how you can create a virtual environment using Python's built-in venv module:

```
python3 -m venv jax-env  # Create a new virtual environment
source jax-env/bin/activate  # Activate the virtual environment
```

Once you're inside your virtual environment, you can install JAX. The JAX team provides pre-built binary wheels for Python 3.7, 3.8, and 3.9 on Linux. You can install JAX using pip:

```
pip install --upgrade pip  # Upgrade pip to the latest version
pip install --upgrade jax jaxlib  # Install JAX and jaxlib
```

This command installs the latest version of JAX that's compatible with your system. If you want to install a specific version of JAX, you can do so by specifying the version number like so:

```
pip install --upgrade jax==VERSION jaxlib==VERSION  # Replace
'VERSION' with the version number
```

Remember to replace VERSION with the version number of JAX that you want to install. Once you've done this, JAX should be installed and ready to use on your CPU! You can verify the installation by opening a Python interpreter and importing JAX:

```
import jax
print(jax.__version__)  # Print the version of JAX to verify the installation
```

If JAX has been installed correctly, this should print the version number of JAX without any errors.

Installing JAX on GPU

Installing JAX with GPU support is slightly more involved than installing it for CPUs. As mentioned earlier, it requires a CUDA-enabled GPU and a compatible version of the CUDA SDK. Additionally, the GPU version of JAX requires the jaxlib package with GPU support.

First, you need to install the CUDA SDK. The exact instructions for doing this can vary depending on your specific system configuration, but in general, the steps are as follows:

- Install the CUDA SDK

- Visit the NVIDIA website and download the installer for the CUDA SDK. JAX supports CUDA 10.1 or later. Be sure to download a version that's compatible with the version of JAX you're planning to install.

- Once you've downloaded the installer, you can install the CUDA SDK by following the instructions provided by NVIDIA.

- Install cuDNN

- After installing the CUDA SDK, you also need to install cuDNN, a GPU-accelerated library for deep neural networks. You can download cuDNN from the NVIDIA website.

- To install cuDNN, you need to extract the downloaded file and copy the resulting files to your CUDA directory. On most Linux systems, the CUDA directory is located at /usr/local/cuda.

Below is how you can install cuDNN:

```
tar -xzvf cudnn-10.1-linux-x64-v7.6.5.32.tgz  # Replace with your downloaded cuDNN file
sudo cp cuda/include/cudnn*.h /usr/local/cuda/include
sudo cp cuda/lib64/libcudnn* /usr/local/cuda/lib64
sudo chmod a+r /usr/local/cuda/include/cudnn*.h
```

/usr/local/cuda/lib64/libcudnn*

- This will install cuDNN to your CUDA directory.

Once you've installed the CUDA SDK and cuDNN, you can install JAX with GPU support.

Below is how you can do it:

- Create and activate a virtual environment (optional but recommended)

```
python3 -m venv jax-env  # Create a new virtual environment
source jax-env/bin/activate  # Activate the virtual environment
```

- Install JAX

```
pip install --upgrade pip  # Upgrade pip to the latest version
pip install --upgrade jax jaxlib==VERSION+cuda101 -f
https://storage.googleapis.com/jax-releases/jax_releases.html  # Install JAX and
jaxlib
```

- In this command, replace VERSION with the version of jaxlib that you want to install. The +cuda101 specifies that you want to install the version of jaxlib with CUDA 10.1 support. If you've installed a different version of the CUDA SDK, you need to adjust this accordingly.

- Verify the installation

You can verify that JAX has been installed correctly by opening a Python interpreter and importing JAX:

```
import jax
print(jax.__version__)  # Print the version of JAX to verify the installation
print(jax.lib.xla_bridge.get_backend().platform)  # Should print 'gpu' if JAX is
correctly set up to use your GPU
```

If JAX has been installed correctly, these commands should print the version number of JAX and gpu, respectively, without any errors.

Tensor Processing Units (TPUs) Deep Dive

Overview

A sort of application-specific integrated circuit (ASIC) designed by Google expressly for the purpose of speeding the workloads associated with machine learning is known as a Tensor Processing Unit (TPU). TPUs are purpose-built to do large numbers of mathematical operations, or, more particularly, tensor operations, in a very efficient manner. Because of this, they are particularly well suited for the applications of deep learning, which entail a great deal of matrix and vector operations, also referred to as tensor operations.

Offloading the intensive computational workloads that are associated with machine learning to a dedicated piece of hardware is the fundamental idea behind TPUs. This allows the central processing unit (CPU) to focus on other activities. TPUs are able to achieve much greater performance and energy efficiency by doing this as opposed to doing the same workloads on a normal CPU or GPU.

You can rent TPU time on a pay-as-you-go basis using Google Cloud's TPU service, which is also available as physical hardware in Google's data centers. In addition, TPUs are also available virtually through this service. TPUs are compatible with a wide range of machine learning frameworks, such as TensorFlow and JAX, and they are able to execute any kind of machine learning model that can be modeled as a computation graph within one of these frameworks. TPUs are also able to be used to train neural networks.

Types of TPUs

Google is notable for being the company that has pushed the bounds of machine learning hardware by releasing four generations of its Tensor Processing Unit (TPU). Each iteration features significant increases in speed, energy efficiency, and performance over the previous generation.

In machine learning, the stage known as "inference" is the point at which the trained model is put to work to generate predictions. The first-generation TPU, also known as TPU v1, was purpose-built to do inference. When it came to the job of serving predictions, the TPU v1 was substantially faster and more energy-efficient than conventional CPUs or GPUs thanks to its specially designed architecture for inference. It also features a bespoke high-speed network that enables rapid communication across several TPU boards. This is an invention that significantly improved its performance and versatility, and it is one of its defining characteristics.

In the second iteration of the TPU, known as the TPU v2 (or TPU v2 Pod), Google extended the capabilities of the TPU so that it now also supports the process of training machine learning models in addition to its original function of serving predictions. The performance of a single TPU v2 device is two times that of its predecessor, the TPU v1, and it comes equipped with 8 GB of high-bandwidth memory. The scalability of the TPU v2 is a characteristic that deserves special mention. These computing units, when combined into powerful "TPU Pods," can give a combined performance of up to 11.5 petaflops when used together. Each TPU Pod can include up to 512 individual TPUs.

The next generation of TPUs, known as the TPU v3 (also known as the TPU v3 Pod), continued the progression of the product line. The TPU v3 had a design that was comparable to the TPU v2, but it provided substantially more power. The performance of a single TPU v3 device can reach up to 100 teraflops, and it comes loaded with 16 gigabytes of high-bandwidth memory. In addition, the TPU v3 may be organized into "TPU Pods," which can include as many as 1,024 TPUs each and produce performance levels of up to 100 petaflops. The requirement for liquid cooling in TPU v3 devices due to their high power output is a significant departure from its predecessors. This is one of the fundamental differences.

The most recent member of the TPU family is the TPU v4, also known as the TPU v4 Pod, which boasts performance capabilities that are twice as powerful as those of the TPU v3. It is capable of delivering performance of up to 260 teraflops and boasts high-bandwidth memory of up to 100 GB/s per TPU. When combined into "TPU Pods," which can include more than 4,000 individual TPUs each, the performance of the TPU v4 can reach up to an astonishing exaflop.

The combination of high performance, large amounts of high-bandwidth memory, and high-speed interconnects make TPUs highly effective for training large, complex machine learning models. This, combined with their availability through Google Cloud, makes TPUs a popular choice for machine learning researchers and practitioners who need to train large models or work with large datasets.

Installing JAX on TPUv4

To use JAX with a TPU, you'll need access to Google Cloud, as TPUs are available only on Google Cloud. To install JAX and the necessary software infrastructure to use TPUs, you can follow these steps:

Create a Google Cloud Project

If you haven't done so already, create a new project on the Google Cloud Platform. do not forget your project has access to TPUs (you may need to enable this in the "APIs and Services" section of your project settings).

Set up Compute Engine VM Instance

You'll need to create a Compute Engine VM instance to run your JAX code. When creating your instance, select an image that has the version of TensorFlow you want to use pre-installed. The TensorFlow version must be compatible with the version of JAX you plan to install.

Also, do not forget to select a zone that has TPU access.

Install JAX and libtpu

Once your VM is set up, you can install JAX and libtpu. First, SSH into your VM:

gcloud compute ssh --project=YOUR_PROJECT_NAME --zone=YOUR_ZONE_NAME YOUR_INSTANCE_NAME

Replace YOUR_PROJECT_NAME, YOUR_ZONE_NAME, and YOUR_INSTANCE_NAME with your project name, zone name, and instance name, respectively.

Then, install JAX and libtpu using pip:

pip install cloud-tpu-client==0.10 https://storage.googleapis.com/jax-releases/jax_releases.html

This will install the cloud TPU client (which includes libtpu) and the version of JAX that's compatible with TPUs.

Verify Installation

Once you've installed JAX and libtpu, you can verify your installation by running a simple JAX program. First, open a Python interpreter:

```
import jax
print(jax.__version__)
print(jax.lib.xla_bridge.get_backend().platform)
```

If everything is set up correctly, this should print the version of JAX and 'tpu'.

If you follow these steps, you should be able to get JAX up and running on a TPU. It is important to keep in mind that running code on a TPU may necessitate some additional settings depending on the particulars of your code and the configuration of your TPU. You should also be aware that employing TPUs will result in additional expenditures on top of the usual fees that are associated with the Google Cloud. Before you begin, you should make it a point to go to the Google Cloud website and look over the pricing information for TPUs there.

Troubleshooting JAX

The installation of JAX can occasionally run into issues due to the variety of environments and hardware it is designed to support - from standard CPUs to more advanced GPUs and TPUs. Below are a few of the most common issues that can arise during the installation process and tips on how to resolve them.

Incompatible Python Version

The first common issue that could cause problems is an incompatible Python version. JAX is designed to work with Python 3.6 or later. If an older version of Python is being used, this could result in installation problems. You can verify your Python version by typing 'python --version' or 'python3 --version' in your terminal. If your Python version is older than 3.6, consider upgrading to a newer version.

Outdated pip

Secondly, having an outdated pip could lead to installation issues. pip is a popular package installer for Python, and having the latest version ensures smooth installation of newer packages. To upgrade pip, you can run 'python -m pip install --upgrade pip' in your terminal.

Incorrect jaxlib Version

Thirdly, using an incorrect version of jaxlib might cause issues when installing JAX for a GPU or TPU. It is essential to ensure that the correct version of jaxlib corresponding to your CUDA/TPU version is installed. Check the CUDA version and make sure you're specifying it correctly when installing jaxlib.

CUDA Installation Issues

Fourthly, CUDA installation issues can arise when installing JAX for use with a GPU. CUDA and cuDNN should be properly installed to enable GPU support. Running 'nvcc --version' should display your CUDA version and 'nvidia-smi' should provide your GPU information. If these commands fail to execute, it may indicate an issue with your CUDA installation.

Errors Importing JAX

Another common issue is errors when importing JAX in Python. If you encounter this, it could indicate a problem with your installation. Try uninstalling and reinstalling JAX and jaxlib by running 'pip uninstall jax jaxlib' and then reinstall them using the correct pip command.

TPU Access

TPU access can also pose a challenge. If you're unable to use a TPU, make sure you've created a Compute Engine VM instance with the correct TPU settings in your Google Cloud project. The VM instance should be in the same zone as the TPU to ensure compatibility.

libtpu not Found

Finally, 'libtpu not found' errors could appear when trying to use a TPU. If you come across this issue, confirm that the 'cloud-tpu-client' package is installed, as it includes libtpu.

Keep in mind that finding solutions to problems frequently involves some degree of trial and error. Whether you are getting a specific error message, it is often beneficial to look for that message on the internet to see whether anyone else has experienced it. It is highly likely that somebody else has run into the same problem, and if they have, they may have found a solution to it that you may use. If all else fails, you always have the option of posting in a relevant online forum and asking for assistance there. Developers are often quite supportive of one another, and it's possible that someone else has encountered and resolved a problem that's comparable to yours.

Integrate JAX into Existing ML

Integrating JAX into an existing Machine Learning project primarily requires you to replace the existing computation and differentiation libraries (like NumPy, SciPy, etc.) with their JAX counterparts. In most cases, the replacement is as simple as changing the import statement. Let us assume we have a simple linear regression project that was originally written using NumPy and SciPy, and you want to switch to JAX.

Below is a step-by-step walkthrough on how to proceed with this:

Identify the Dependencies

Look through your code and identify which parts are dependent on NumPy, SciPy, or any other libraries that you plan to replace with JAX.

For example, you might have a linear regression model using the normal equation method in NumPy as follows:

```
import numpy as np

# Hypothetical X and y for demonstration
X = np.random.rand(100, 1)
y = 2 + 3 * X + np.random.rand(100, 1)

# Adding bias
X_b = np.c_[np.ones((100, 1)), X]

theta_best = np.linalg.inv(X_b.T.dot(X_b)).dot(X_b.T).dot(y)
```

Replace the Dependencies with JAX

Replace the import statements for the libraries you're replacing with import statements for the JAX equivalents. For NumPy, this will be jax.numpy:

```
import jax.numpy as jnp
from jax import random
```

```
key = random.PRNGKey(0)

# Hypothetical X and y for demonstration
X = random.normal(key, (100, 1))
y = 2 + 3 * X + random.normal(key, (100, 1))

# Adding bias
X_b = jnp.column_stack((jnp.ones((100, 1)), X))

theta_best = jnp.linalg.inv(X_b.T.dot(X_b)).dot(X_b.T).dot(y)
```

Note: When replacing numpy with jax.numpy, keep in mind that JAX arrays are immutable, which is not the case with NumPy arrays.

Test the Code

After replacing the dependencies, test the code to ensure that it still runs as expected. If there are any issues, you may need to modify the code further to accommodate the specifics of JAX. For instance, if your code relies on in-place mutations of arrays (which NumPy supports but JAX doesn't), you'll have to refactor that code.

Replace the Gradient Computations

If your code computes gradients, you'll need to replace those computations with JAX's automatic differentiation. For instance, suppose you had a function that computed the gradient of a loss function for your model. With JAX, you can compute this using the grad function:

```
from jax import grad

# Suppose we have some loss function
def loss_fn(theta, X, y):
    return jnp.mean((jnp.dot(X, theta) - y) ** 2)

# We can compute its gradient with respect to theta as follows
grad_loss_fn = grad(loss_fn)
```

Replace Optimizers

If your code includes an optimizer, you'll need to replace it with one that can handle JAX arrays. JAX has built-in support for many common optimizers in the jax.experimental.optimizers module.

```
from jax.experimental import optimizers

# Suppose we want to use gradient descent
opt_init, opt_update, get_params = optimizers.sgd(step_size=0.1)

# We can then use these functions to perform optimization
opt_state = opt_init(theta)

for i in range(num_steps):
    grads = grad_loss_fn(get_params(opt_state), X, y)
    opt_state = opt_update(i, grads, opt_state)

theta = get_params(opt_state)
```

Transitioning from libraries like NumPy to JAX can be both exciting and challenging due to the impressive capabilities that JAX brings to the table, such as auto-differentiation and easy parallelization. However, it's essential to be mindful that this shift can result in differences in behavior due to the distinct design philosophy and implementation of JAX. For example, JAX's core idea is to be functionally pure as much as possible, meaning it avoids side-effects that could occur in other libraries. Functions that operate on arrays in JAX will return new arrays and won't modify existing ones. This is contrary to NumPy, where some operations might change the contents of the array in-place. This difference can lead to unexpected results if not properly considered during the transition process.

Integrating JAX into TensorFlow Project

Integrating JAX into an existing complex ML project, which might be using TensorFlow or similar libraries, needs a careful approach due to some intrinsic differences between TensorFlow and JAX. The changes will often not be as simple as just replacing import statements, and some modifications to the code logic may be needed.

Below is a step-by-step walkthrough on how to proceed with integrating JAX into a TensorFlow project.

Identify the Dependencies

The first step will be to identify where your project is using TensorFlow for tasks that JAX can handle. This could be anything from basic numerical computation and matrix operations to gradient computation and optimization.

Replace TensorFlow with JAX

The next step would be to replace the TensorFlow parts of your code with equivalent JAX code. Below is an example of how to translate a simple TensorFlow operation to JAX:

TensorFlow code:

```
import tensorflow as tf

# Create a random tensor
tf_x = tf.random.normal((10,))

# Compute the square of the tensor
tf_y = tf.square(tf_x)
```

Equivalent JAX code:

```
from jax import random

# Create a random array
key = random.PRNGKey(0)
jax_x = random.normal(key, (10,))

# Compute the square of the array
jax_y = jax_x ** 2
```

When doing this, keep in mind that some TensorFlow functions may not have direct equivalents in JAX. For example, TensorFlow's placeholders and session-based execution model do not have direct equivalents in JAX.

Replace TensorFlow Gradient Computations

If your TensorFlow code computes gradients, you can replace this with JAX's grad function. Below is an example of how to translate TensorFlow's gradient computation to JAX:

TensorFlow code:

```
x = tf.Variable(3.0)
with tf.GradientTape() as tape:
    y = tf.square(x)
dy_dx = tape.gradient(y, x)
```

Equivalent JAX code:

```
from jax import grad

x = 3.0
y = lambda x: x ** 2
dy_dx = grad(y)(x)
```

Note that unlike TensorFlow, JAX computes gradients with respect to function inputs directly rather than with respect to variables in the computational graph. This is because JAX operates on a function-based computation model rather than a graph-based model.

Replace TensorFlow Optimizers

If your TensorFlow code uses TensorFlow's built-in optimizers, you can replace this with optimizers from jax.experimental.optimizers. Below is an example of how to translate TensorFlow's optimizer usage to JAX:

TensorFlow code:

```
var = tf.Variable(3.0)
```

```
loss = lambda: var ** 2  # some arbitrary loss function
opt = tf.keras.optimizers.SGD(learning_rate=0.1)
opt.minimize(loss, var_list=[var])
```

Equivalent JAX code:

```
from jax import value_and_grad
from jax.experimental import optimizers

var = 3.0
loss = lambda var: var ** 2  # some arbitrary loss function
opt_init, opt_update, get_params = optimizers.sgd(0.1)


opt_state = opt_init(var)

value, grads = value_and_grad(loss)(get_params(opt_state))
opt_state = opt_update(0, grads, opt_state)
var = get_params(opt_state)
```

Test the Code

After transitioning to JAX, do not forget to validate the results. Any subtle differences in the way TensorFlow and JAX handle computations can potentially lead to differences in the final outcomes. Always check the outputs and make sure the model is still performing as expected.

While transitioning an existing TensorFlow project to JAX can be a non-trivial task due to differences in the computation models of the two libraries, it can often lead to more efficient and easily understandable code, due to JAX's function-based computation model and powerful features like just-in-time compilation and automatic differentiation.

Integrating JAX into PyTorch Deep Learning

The process of integrating JAX into an existing PyTorch deep learning project follows a method that is comparable to that of TensorFlow; however, given the differences between PyTorch and JAX, there are additional specific elements to take into consideration.

Below is a step-by-step walkthrough on how to integrate JAX into a PyTorch deep learning project:

Identify the Dependencies

Similar to the TensorFlow case, you'll need to identify where your project is using PyTorch for tasks that JAX can handle, such as array computation, differentiation, and optimization.

Replace PyTorch with JAX

Replace the PyTorch parts of your code with equivalent JAX code. For instance, if you're using PyTorch for array computation and matrix operations:

PyTorch code:

```
import torch

# Create a tensor
torch_x = torch.randn((10,))

# Compute the square of the tensor
torch_y = torch_x.pow(2)
```

Equivalent JAX code:

```
from jax import random

# Create a random array
key = random.PRNGKey(0)
jax_x = random.normal(key, (10,))

# Compute the square of the array
jax_y = jax_x ** 2
```

Replace PyTorch Gradient Computations

If your PyTorch code computes gradients, you can replace this with JAX's grad function. For example:

PyTorch code:

```
x = torch.tensor(3.0, requires_grad=True)
y = x.pow(2)
y.backward()
dy_dx = x.grad
```

Equivalent JAX code:

```
from jax import grad

x = 3.0
y = lambda x: x ** 2
dy_dx = grad(y)(x)
```

Replace PyTorch Optimizers

PyTorch has its built-in optimizers in torch.optim. JAX has equivalent optimizers in jax.experimental.optimizers.

PyTorch code:

```
import torch.optim as optim

var = torch.tensor(3.0, requires_grad=True)
optimizer = optim.SGD([var], lr=0.1)

def step():
    var_sq = var.pow(2)
    var_sq.backward()
```

```
    optimizer.step()
    optimizer.zero_grad()

step()
```

Equivalent JAX code:

```
from jax import value_and_grad
from jax.experimental import optimizers

var = 3.0
opt_init, opt_update, get_params = optimizers.sgd(0.1)
opt_state = opt_init(var)

def step(i, opt_state):
    value, grads = value_and_grad(lambda x: x ** 2)(get_params(opt_state))
    return opt_update(i, grads, opt_state)

opt_state = step(0, opt_state)
var = get_params(opt_state)
```

Test the Code

After you have made these modifications, you should run your code to check that it is still able to deliver the desired outcomes. There may be some minute variations in the manner in which operations are carried out due to the fact that JAX uses a function-based computation model, whereas PyTorch makes use of a dynamic computational graph model.

Keep in mind that the process of transitioning may require you to make some modifications to the way that you arrange your code, particularly if you are making use of the dynamic computation graph feature that PyTorch offers. In these kinds of circumstances, you will need to rewrite your code so that it can function within the more functional and static computational paradigm that JAX provides.

Summary

In this chapter, we explored deep into the process of installing JAX into machine learning and deep learning projects and integrating it into those projects. To begin, we became familiar with the requirements for installing JAX on a variety of hardware configurations, such as CPU, GPU, and TPU. For example, JAX is dependent on particular libraries and drivers, such as CUDA and cuDNN for GPUs and libtpu for TPUs. In addition, the installation procedure for Linux was detailed, including the Python instructions and environment parameters that were required.

Tensor Processing Units (TPUs), which are application-specific integrated circuits (ASICs) developed by Google and utilized to accelerate the workloads associated with machine learning, were discussed in greater depth throughout this chapter. They are developed to offer the highest possible levels of performance and efficiency. We went over the many generations of the TPU, their performance characteristics, and how to make use of TPUs with the JAX programming language. In addition, a step-by-step walkthrough was presented for installing JAX on TPUs, which covered the management of required dependencies like libtpu and TensorFlow.

Lastly, we investigated ways to include JAX into existing machine learning applications, with a particular emphasis on those based on TensorFlow and PyTorch. The chapter drew attention to the fundamental distinctions that exist between these libraries as well as the ways in which these distinctions influence the transition procedure. Several characteristics of TensorFlow, like as placeholders and the session-based execution mechanism, were called out as lacking a clear analogue in JAX. These aspects were highlighted. PyTorch's shift to JAX's functional and static computational model from PyTorch's dynamic computational graph model required extensive attention to transitional details. The procedures for replacing fundamental computation, gradient computation, and optimization with JAX's counterparts were outlined, with an emphasis placed on the importance of confirming findings after the transition had taken place. This chapter takes a methodical approach to addressing topics such as the installation of JAX, an understanding of TPUs, and the incorporation of JAX into already existing projects.

CHAPTER 4: JAX FOR NUMERICAL COMPUTING: THE BASICS

Advanced Numerical Operations of JAX

JAX enhances the capabilities of traditional numerical computing libraries like NumPy by offering a host of advanced numerical operations. These operations are tailored to maximize performance, precision, and adaptability, making JAX an effective tool for large-scale scientific computations and machine learning applications.

Advanced Indexing

Advanced indexing in JAX is a versatile tool that greatly enhances the capacity of data scientists and machine learning engineers to manipulate and operate on multi-dimensional data structures. This ability to perform integer array indexing, boolean array indexing, and index array broadcasting facilitates intricate data operations. For instance, one can filter elements from an array based on conditions, reorder elements, or even use one array as an index to another, thereby enabling intricate reshaping and manipulation of data structures. These features, particularly when used in complex machine learning or data analysis pipelines, can dramatically simplify the codebase, improving its maintainability and readability.

JAX JIT Compilation for Numerical Operations

The just-in-time (JIT) compilation offered by JAX is a defining feature that sets it apart from traditional numerical libraries. By employing the jax.jit function, Python code that contains numerical operations can be compiled into highly optimized machine code during runtime. This JIT compilation reduces the interpretational overhead typically associated with Python, delivering a substantial performance boost. This speed-up is particularly pronounced in cases where the JIT-compiled function encapsulates large-scale computations or when the function is invoked repeatedly. The end result is a significant reduction in the execution time, making JAX highly attractive for numerical computing tasks, particularly those in the realm of machine learning and data analysis.

Batched Operations (vmap)

In addition to JIT compilation, JAX provides another powerful tool for optimizing numerical computations in the form of vectorized, or batched, operations. Leveraging the jax.vmap function, a user can automatically vectorize a function across a specified dimension. In practical terms, this means that one can avoid writing explicit for-loops in their code, a feature that often leads to a slowdown in numerical computing languages. Instead, jax.vmap is capable of implicitly looping over the input data, leading to faster and more efficient computations. This is particularly advantageous when dealing with operations on large arrays, where the efficiency gains from vectorization can be substantial.

Furthermore, the ability to specify the dimension along which the vectorization occurs gives the user an additional layer of control and flexibility, allowing them to optimize their computations for their specific use case.

Automatic Differentiation of Numerical Functions

In any realm that deals with numerical computation, especially machine learning, automatic differentiation plays a crucial role. The process of automatic differentiation essentially involves calculating the derivatives of numeric functions without any need for manual differentiation. This capability is key to several machine learning algorithms, most importantly in neural network training. JAX's grad function is an automatic differentiation tool that allows easy computation of gradients. It also facilitates computing Jacobians via jacfwd and jacrev functions and Hessians through the hessian function, making it a useful tool for more complex optimization tasks.

Complex Numbers and Derivatives

In addition to these, JAX extends a comprehensive support for complex numbers. Complex numbers are widely used in various areas of computation such as quantum computing and signal processing. JAX enables arithmetic operations with these complex numbers, allows computation of their absolute values, their real or imaginary parts, and their gradients, providing a useful platform for handling complex numerical operations.

Support for Custom Gradient Functions

Custom gradient functions often become a necessity when the standard ways of computing gradients aren't optimal or not feasible. In such scenarios, JAX comes equipped with the jax.custom_grad function that allows the definition of custom gradient functions. This offers you an enhanced control over the computation, making the implementation of advanced optimization algorithms a possibility.

Control Flow

Native Python control flow statements, including if, for, while, etc., have functional alternatives in JAX – jax.lax.cond, jax.lax.scan, and jax.lax.while_loop. These alternatives make possible the implementation of differentiable, JIT-compilable operations on tensor-like variables with conditional statements and loops.

Efficient Linear Algebra Operations

Efficient linear algebra operations are at the heart of machine learning computations. JAX offers an array of optimized linear algebra operations for performance enhancement. This includes matrix multiplication, matrix-vector product, Cholesky decomposition, QR decomposition, singular value decomposition, and many more.

Lastly, a critical part of using JAX is understanding the unique behavior it can exhibit due to its functional programming philosophy and the way it handles array updates. It becomes essential to validate the results thoroughly after transitioning your code to JAX. Overall, JAX is a powerful tool with several advanced features that can greatly accelerate numerical computations and machine learning tasks.

Advanced Indexing

Accessing or changing intricate data patterns stored in array-like structures is the focus of advanced indexing in both JAX and NumPy. Advanced indexing allows users to do this. It opens up more possibilities in addition to the conventional indexing methods of integers or slices. JAX is capable of supporting all of the sophisticated indexing methods that are available in NumPy. These methods include indexing integer arrays, indexing boolean arrays, and broadcasting over one array in order to index another array.

Consider the following for a more in-depth examination:

Integer Array Indexing

Integer array indexing is a powerful feature in array-based computing and numerical libraries like NumPy. It enables you to create new arrays from an existing one based on a set of indices. This technique is highly flexible and allows for the construction of complex data structures in a straightforward way.

Let us explore this concept through an example:

```
import jax.numpy as jnp

a = jnp.array([[1, 2], [3, 4], [5, 6]])

# An example of integer array indexing.
print(a[[0, 1, 2], [0, 1, 0]])  # Prints "[1 4 5]"
```

Here, the elements at (0,0), (1,1), and (2,0) are being selected. Integer array indexing can be handy when you want to select or modify certain elements from an array without changing its shape or other elements.

Boolean Array Indexing

Boolean array indexing is a powerful tool in Python programming, particularly within libraries like NumPy, that enables selective data access. In essence, this form of indexing allows you to pick arbitrary elements of an array based on a certain condition or a set of conditions.

To illustrate, let us imagine we have an array of numbers and we want to select all elements that are greater than a certain value. This is where Boolean array indexing comes into play.

Consider this example:

```
import jax.numpy as jnp

a = jnp.array([[1, 2], [3, 4], [5, 6]])

# Find the elements of a that are bigger than 2;
# this returns a boolean array of the same shape as a.
bool_idx = (a > 2)
print(bool_idx)  # Prints "[[False False] [ True  True] [ True  True]]"

# Use boolean array indexing to construct a rank 1 array
# consisting of the elements of a corresponding to the True values
# of bool_idx
print(a[bool_idx])  # Prints "[3 4 5 6]"
```

The most common application of this method is to pick or modify members of an array depending on a set of criteria in a conditional fashion using this technique. Keep in mind that, in contrast to simple indexing, advanced indexing will invariably produce a copy of the data. In addition, repeating indices during advanced indexing could provide surprising results, in contrast to how NumPy handles things, which allows for it.

When working with multidimensional data, advanced indexing can be a useful tool because it enables more complex data manipulation than simple indexing or conventional slicing does. Developers are able to produce code that is cleaner and easier to read when they make use of advanced indexing.

JAX JIT Compilation for Numerical Operations

JAX's jax.jit function is a mechanism for speeding up your code by compiling it Just-In-Time. It stands for "just-in-time" compilation and it's a way of improving the execution speed of Python functions that perform numerical computations.

In essence, it works by tracing the function, capturing the operations as it goes, and compiling this operation sequence into highly efficient machine code. The resulting machine code is specialized to the specific shapes and types of the input arrays, so it runs much faster than the interpreted Python code.

It's crucial to note that not all Python features are supported inside JIT-compiled functions. Anything that isn't related to the numerical computations (like print statements or file I/O) will be run at compile-time, not at run-time, which is often not what you want. Also, control flow that depends on the values of the input arrays has to be expressed using special JAX primitives, like jax.lax.cond and jax.lax.while_loop.

Sample Program on using JAX.JIT

Below is an example of using jax.jit to speed up a function that performs a large amount of computation:

```
import jax
import jax.numpy as jnp

def slow_function(x):
    # A function that does a large amount of computation
    result = x
    for _ in range(10000):
        result = result + x ** 2 + x ** 3
    return result

# Jit-compile the function to make it run faster
fast_function = jax.jit(slow_function)
```

```
x = jnp.array([1, 2, 3, 4, 5])

# Call the slow function and measure the time
import time
start = time.time()
print(slow_function(x))
print("Time for slow function:", time.time() - start)

# Call the fast function and measure the time
start = time.time()
print(fast_function(x))
print("Time for fast function:", time.time() - start)
```

In the given example, we witness the benefits of jit-compiled functions, as they demonstrate considerably higher execution speed in comparison to their non-jit counterparts, despite performing the exact same computations. However, one must bear in mind that the jax.jit function isn't a miraculous tool that universally accelerates all functions. Its efficacy is most noticeable in the context of functions heavily engaged in numerical computations.

In scenarios where a function already exhibits fast execution or its operations predominantly involve tasks other than numerical computations, such as file input/output, the utilization of jit-compilation might not yield a significant enhancement in speed. The judicious application of jax.jit can therefore lead to substantial optimization in certain circumstances, but is not a universally applicable solution for performance improvement.

Batched Operations

The jax.vmap function is another powerful tool provided by JAX for high performance computation. It stands for vectorized map and it can automatically vectorize a function, i.e., it transforms a function that operates on single data points to one that operates on batches of data points. This process is extremely efficient and significantly faster than manually looping over the batch dimension.

The function jax.vmap essentially transforms a function $f(x)$ that acts on a single data point x into a function $f'(X)$ that acts on a batch of data points X. $f'(X)$ produces the same output as map(f, X), but it shares computation across all the data points in the batch, making it much faster.

The given below is a simplified example:

```
import jax
import jax.numpy as jnp

# Below is a function that operates on single data points
def f(x):
    return jnp.sin(x) ** 2 + jnp.cos(x) ** 2

x = jnp.linspace(0, 10, 1000)  # A large batch of data points

# Without vmap, we would have to use a loop or a comprehension to apply f to
each data point individually
y_slow = jnp.array([f(xi) for xi in x])

# With vmap, we can vectorize the computation in one line
y_fast = jax.vmap(f)(x)

# The outputs are the same
print(jnp.allclose(y_slow, y_fast))  # Prints: True
```

In the above sample program, using jax.vmap makes the computation significantly faster, because it avoids the overhead of Python loops and allows JAX to parallelize the computation.

Moreover, jax.vmap can be combined with jax.jit for even greater speedups. The jax.jit function will compile the computation into efficient machine code, and jax.vmap will share this computation across all the data points in the batch. Below is how you can do this:

```
# Combine vmap and jit for maximum performance
fast_f = jax.jit(jax.vmap(f))
y_super_fast = fast_f(x)

# The output is the same
```

```
print(jnp.allclose(y_slow, y_super_fast))  # Prints: True
```

In summary, jax.vmap is a powerful tool for vectorizing computations, making them run faster and allowing them to operate on batches of data. It is especially useful for computations that are naturally expressed in terms of operations on single data points, but need to be performed on large batches of data for efficiency.

Automatic Differentiation for ML

Automatic distinction is among the most significant capabilities that JAX has to offer. This feature is crucial for machine learning since it enables the calculation of gradients. Gradients are then used to optimize model parameters while the model is being trained, therefore having this feature is essential. The jax.grad function is at the heart of JAX's automatic differentiation capabilities.

The jax.grad function calculates the function's gradient. In other words, if you provide jax.grad(f) a function, it will return another function that calculates the gradient of f with respect to its inputs.

Below is a simple example:

```
import jax

def f(x):
    return jax.numpy.sin(x) ** 2

grad_f = jax.grad(f)
print(grad_f(1.0))  # should print "-0.9092974", which is the derivative of sin^2(x)
at x = 1
```

In addition to jax.grad, JAX provides jax.jacfwd and jax.jacrev for computing the Jacobian of a function. The Jacobian is a matrix that contains all the first-order partial derivatives of a function. jax.jacfwd computes the Jacobian using forward-mode autodiff, while jax.jacrev computes it using reverse-mode.

Now, let us consider a more complicated example: using jax.grad to compute the gradient of a loss function for a simple machine learning model. We'll consider a linear regression model, where the goal is to fit a line to a set of points.

```python
import jax
import jax.numpy as jnp

# Our simple model is just a linear function
def model(params, x):
    return jnp.dot(params, x)

# The loss function is the mean squared error between the model's predictions
# and the true values
def loss(params, x, y_true):
    y_pred = model(params, x)
    return jnp.mean((y_pred - y_true) ** 2)

# Initialize the model parameters
params = jnp.array([0.0, 0.0])

# Some example data
x = jnp.array([1.0, 2.0, 3.0, 4.0, 5.0])
y_true = jnp.array([2.0, 4.0, 6.0, 8.0, 10.0])

# Compute the gradient of the loss function
grad_loss = jax.grad(loss)

# The returned function grad_loss takes the same arguments as the original
# function loss
grads = grad_loss(params, x, y_true)

# grads is a vector of the same size as params, containing the derivatives of the
# loss with respect to each parameter
print(grads)
```

This example demonstrates how to compute gradients using JAX. This is typically how you would use JAX in a machine learning setting: define your model and loss function, then use jax.grad to compute the gradient of the loss with respect to the model parameters. You can then use these gradients to update the model parameters, for example using gradient descent.

Using JAX for Custom Gradient

In addition to its capabilities for automatic differentiation, JAX also provides powerful tools for defining custom gradients. This can be useful when the standard gradient isn't the one you want (for example, in certain cases with discontinuities), or when the standard gradient is numerically unstable.

To define a custom gradient, you can use the jax.custom_grad function. This function takes as input a function f for which you want to define a custom gradient. You provide another function that computes the forward pass and the custom backward pass. Below is an example:

```
import jax
import jax.numpy as jnp

def tanh(x):
    y = jnp.tanh(x)
    def grad_fn(g):
        # grad of tanh is (1 - y^2)
        return g * (1 - y**2)
    return y, grad_fn

tanh_custom_grad = jax.custom_grad(tanh)

# Now tanh_custom_grad can be used like a standard JAX function with
automatic gradients
x = jnp.array([1.0, 2.0, 3.0])
print(jax.grad(tanh_custom_grad)(x))  # should print [0.4199743 0.07065082
0.00986604]
```

In the above sample program, tanh_custom_grad computes the tanh function and its gradient. The grad_fn function defined inside tanh is the custom gradient function. It takes as input a scalar g which is the "incoming" gradient from the computation following the tanh operation. It then multiplies this incoming gradient with the derivative of the tanh function, (1 - y**2), to compute the outgoing gradient.

The jax.custom_grad function allows you to define complex custom gradient functions that can handle cases where the standard automatic differentiation would fail or produce undesired results. However, it requires a good understanding of the underlying mathematics and should be used with caution. Incorrect gradients can lead to subtle bugs and incorrect results in your machine learning algorithms.

JAX for Python's Control Flow

JAX does indeed support Python's native control flow statements (if, for, while) and provides its own functions for more efficient control flow operations: jax.lax.cond, jax.lax.scan, and jax.lax.while_loop. These functions are designed to be used within JIT-compiled functions and provide efficient execution in the compiled code.

Jax.lax.cond

This is a conditional function equivalent to 'if-else' in python. It takes three required functions (true_fun, false_fun, pred) and two arguments (true_operand, false_operand). Depending upon the boolean value of pred, it applies either true_fun or false_fun to the corresponding operand.

```
import jax
from jax import lax

def f(x):
    return lax.cond(x < 0,
            lambda _: 0.0,  # function to return if condition is true
            lambda y: y,  # function to return if condition is false
            operand=x)  # the operand to pass to the chosen function

print(f(1.0))  # Prints: 1.0
print(f(-1.0))  # Prints: 0.0
```

Jax.lax.while_loop

This function allows us to write loops inside a JIT-compiled function. It's similar to Python's while loop but is efficient when JIT compiled.

```
def sum_first_n(n):
    def cond_fun(carry):
        i, _ = carry
        return i <= n

    def body_fun(carry):
        i, total = carry
        return i + 1, total + i

    init_val = (0, 0)
    _, total = lax.while_loop(cond_fun, body_fun, init_val)
    return total


# JIT compile the function for better performance
jit_sum_first_n = jax.jit(sum_first_n)


print(jit_sum_first_n(5))  # Prints: 15
```

Jax.lax.scan

This function is used to express loops over the leading axis of arrays. It is particularly useful when JIT compiling, as Python's for loop is not JIT-compatible.

```
import jax.numpy as jnp


def cumulative_sum(x):
    def body_fun(carry, x):
        total = carry + x
        return total, total
```

```
    _, y = lax.scan(body_fun, 0.0, x)
    return y

# JIT compile the function for better performance
jit_cumulative_sum = jax.jit(cumulative_sum)

print(jit_cumulative_sum(jnp.array([1, 2, 3, 4, 5])))  # Prints: [ 1.  3.  6. 10. 15.]
```

These are just brief examples. lax.cond, lax.while_loop, and lax.scan are all highly flexible and can be used to construct complex control flow structures.

Summary

In this chapter, we went over some of the more advanced numerical capabilities that JAX offers. We started by taking a look at advanced indexing, which enables operations to be carried out on a subset of array items. Advanced indexing is an essential component of numerical computing, and JAX enhances the capabilities of classic NumPy beyond what they were previously capable of.

Following this, we conducted an in-depth investigation of the just-in-time (JIT) compilation feature that is available in JAX. This feature transforms Python and JAX code into effective machine code. As an example program demonstrates, this results in a speed increase for the execution of the program, particularly for computations of a big scale. Following that, we investigated batch processing by utilizing the jax.vmap function for automatic vectorization. This allowed us to demonstrate JAX's capability of doing computations on high-dimensional data in an effective manner. We also gained an understanding of how JAX provides support for automated distinction, which is an important component of machine learning. For the purpose of computing gradients and Jacobians, we investigated the jax.grad, jax.jacfwd, and jax.jacrev functions. In addition to that, we talked about the jax.custom_grad function, which allows users to define their own unique gradients. This can be an essential component for specific categories of mathematical functions or for achieving greater numerical stability. After that, we investigated how JAX can deal with the control flow in native Python as well as the more effective JAX alternatives such as jax.lax.cond, jax.lax.scan, and jax.lax.while_loop.

In general, this chapter did a good job of providing a comprehensive grasp of JAX's advanced numerical operations. It also did a good job of demonstrating the power and flexibility of JAX for scientific computing and machine learning. The capabilities and functionalities that are going to be described in this chapter establish JAX as a flexible tool that can be used for both small scale computations and big scale machine learning applications that require high performance.

Chapter 5: Diving Deeper into Auto-Differentiation and Gradients

Auto-Differentiation and Gradients in JAX

JAX distinguishes itself through first-rate features such as automatic differentiation, a powerful tool in high-performance machine learning research. This section will delve into the intricacies of automatic differentiation, highlight new functions designed for gradient computations, and elucidate how these can be applied in diverse scenarios. Although the previous section briefly touched upon the grad function, this part aims to provide a more comprehensive understanding of automatic differentiation.

To effectively use JAX, a robust grasp of automatic differentiation is crucial. It's important to note that this concept deviates from numerical and symbolic differentiation. Automatic differentiation represents a unique method that leverages the computational graph of a function to compute derivatives in an efficient and precise manner.

Beyond the scope of simple gradients, JAX provides the jax.jacfwd and jax.jacrev functions for computing the Jacobian matrix of a function, along with the jax.hessian function for the Hessian matrix. Jacobians are particularly useful when dealing with functions that handle vector inputs and outputs, whereas Hessians, the second-order derivatives, find frequent use in optimization algorithms.

When tackling machine learning challenges, we often confront functions that accept input vectors. Thankfully, JAX is equipped with built-in support for these functions, facilitating the handling of complex machine learning tasks. Nested grad calls in JAX offer a convenient tool for computing higher-order derivatives, enabling the calculation of second or third-order derivatives. This proves invaluable for algorithms that necessitate such derivatives.

A standout feature of JAX's automatic differentiation is its compatibility with Python's native control flow statements, thus simplifying the computation of gradients for functions involving conditional (if/else) statements and loops. JAX empowers users to define their own gradients for the functions they create, catering to intricate scenarios where standard gradient computations fail or lack efficiency. It's common to encounter zero or NaN gradients during the training of neural networks. Understanding the cause of these occurrences, and more importantly, how to manage them, is crucial. Gradients form the bedrock of optimization in machine learning models. We'll explore how to harness JAX's gradient computations for optimization issues, particularly in training neural networks.

In subsequent sections, we will dive deeper into these topics, supplementing theoretical explanations with real-world examples and code snippets, thereby demonstrating the practical implementation of JAX's robust auto-differentiation capabilities.

Computing Derivatives using Computational Graphs

Automatic differentiation is a core concept in the computational backends of many machine learning frameworks, including JAX. Automatic differentiation is a method to compute the derivative of a function specified by a computer program. It leverages the computational graph of a function to compute derivatives accurately and efficiently.

To understand automatic differentiation, let us first understand what a computational graph is. A computational graph is a directed graph where nodes correspond to operations or variables. Variables can be input to the function, or they can be intermediate values created during the execution of the function. Operations can be any kind of function or mathematical operation.

To illustrate, let us consider a simple function:

```python
def f(x, y):
    return x ** 2 + y ** 2
```

Here, nodes are operations (**2 and +), and edges are the variables (x, y, and the intermediate values).

Automatic differentiation computes the derivatives by traversing this graph from the output back to the inputs, applying the chain rule to compute derivatives along the way.

JAX can automatically compute these derivatives for us using the grad function:

```python
from jax import grad
import jax.numpy as jnp

def f(x, y):
    return jnp.sum(x ** 2 + y ** 2)

x = jnp.array([2.0, 3.0])
y = jnp.array([1.0, -1.0])
```

```
grad_f_x = grad(f, argnums=0)  # get gradient w.r.t. x
grad_f_y = grad(f, argnums=1)  # get gradient w.r.t. y

print("Gradient of f w.r.t. x:", grad_f_x(x, y))
print("Gradient of f w.r.t. y:", grad_f_y(x, y))
```

Output:

```
Gradient of f w.r.t. x: [4. 6.]
Gradient of f w.r.t. y: [2. -2.]
```

The grad function in JAX returns a new function that computes the derivative of the original function. We can specify which argument we want to compute the gradient with respect to using the argnums parameter. In the code above, grad_f_x computes the gradient of f with respect to x, and grad_f_y computes the gradient of f with respect to y.

This is a simplified example, but the power of automatic differentiation in JAX is that it can handle complex functions with multiple operations and branches. It also extends beyond scalar functions to vector functions with the use of the Jacobian and Hessian.

Jacobians and Hessians Matrix

Let us start with the concept of Jacobians and Hessians in the context of Automatic Differentiation:

Jacobian

The Jacobian matrix, named after Carl Gustav Jacob Jacobi, is a matrix of all first-order partial derivatives of a vector-valued function. The Jacobian of a function gives you the gradients of a function with respect to all of its inputs. In simple terms, the Jacobian matrix helps to capture how changes in the inputs affect the changes in the outputs.

Hessian

The Hessian matrix, named after the German mathematician Ludwig Otto Hessian, is a square matrix of second-order partial derivatives of a scalar-valued function, or scalar field. The Hessian essentially gives us information about the curvature of the function at a given point.

In JAX, we have jax.jacfwd and jax.jacrev for computing the Jacobian matrix, and jax.hessian for computing the Hessian matrix.

Now, let us delve into an example:

Let us consider we have a function f: R^2 -> R^2 (a function with two inputs and two outputs), defined as:

```
def f(x):
    return jnp.array([x[0] ** 2, x[1] ** 3])
```

Now, if we want to compute the Jacobian of this function, we can use jax.jacfwd or jax.jacrev:

```
from jax import jacfwd, jacrev

# define our function
def f(x):
    return jnp.array([x[0] ** 2, x[1] ** 3])

x = jnp.array([2.0, 3.0])  # some input

# compute Jacobian using forward-mode differentiation
jacobian_f_fwd = jacfwd(f)
print("Jacobian (forward-mode):", jacobian_f_fwd(x))

# compute Jacobian using reverse-mode differentiation
jacobian_f_rev = jacrev(f)
print("Jacobian (reverse-mode):", jacobian_f_rev(x))
```

The choice between jax.jacfwd and jax.jacrev depends on the shape of your input and output. If your function has many inputs and fewer outputs, jax.jacrev is likely to be faster, and vice versa.

Now, let us compute the Hessian of a function g: R^2 -> R, defined as:

```
def g(x):
    return x[0] ** 2 + x[1] ** 4
```

The Hessian matrix of this function can be computed as follows:

```
from jax import hessian

# define our function
def g(x):
    return x[0] ** 2 + x[1] ** 4

x = jnp.array([2.0, 3.0])  # some input

# compute Hessian
hessian_g = hessian(g)
print("Hessian:", hessian_g(x))
```

Here, the jax.hessian function computes the Hessian matrix of the function g at the point x.

Compute Higher-order Derivatives

JAX provides a unique advantage by allowing us to compute higher-order derivatives. This can be achieved through nesting calls to the grad function.

A higher-order derivative is simply a derivative of a derivative. For instance, the second-order derivative of a function f(x) is the derivative of its first derivative. These derivatives can provide useful insights about the function. For example, the second derivative can tell us whether the function is convex or concave.

In JAX, to compute higher order derivatives, you can simply call the grad function multiple times, where each call computes the derivative of the previous. This is known as nested differentiation.

Let us consider a simple function:

```
def f(x):
    return x ** 3 + 2 * x ** 2 - 3 * x + 1
```

The first derivative of this function can be computed as follows:

```
f_prime = grad(f)  # computes the first derivative of f
```

To compute the second derivative (also known as the second order derivative), you can call grad again on the first derivative:

```
f_double_prime = grad(f_prime)  # computes the second derivative of f
```

Similarly, for the third derivative:

```
f_triple_prime = grad(f_double_prime)  # computes the third derivative of f
```

The given below is a complete example:

```
from jax import grad
import jax.numpy as jnp

def f(x):
    return x ** 3 + 2 * x ** 2 - 3 * x + 1

x = jnp.array([2.0])  # some input

# compute first derivative
f_prime = grad(f)
print("First derivative at x = 2.0:", f_prime(x))

# compute second derivative
f_double_prime = grad(f_prime)
print("Second derivative at x = 2.0:", f_double_prime(x))
```

```
# compute third derivative
f_triple_prime = grad(f_double_prime)
print("Third derivative at x = 2.0:", f_triple_prime(x))
```

Note that higher-order derivatives are often less stable numerically, because each differentiation operation can amplify errors or introduce noise. It is often beneficial to try and reformulate your problem so that only first-order derivatives are required. However, in cases where higher order derivatives are necessary, JAX makes it possible to compute them efficiently and easily.

Handling Zero and NaN Gradients

In machine learning and deep learning, you might occasionally encounter zero or NaN (not a number) gradients. These are special cases in gradient-based optimization and can sometimes cause problems.

Zero Gradients

Zero gradients can occur when the derivative of a function at a given point is zero. For example, at the minimum or maximum of a function, the derivative is zero. In a neural network, zero gradients can occur due to the choice of activation function, or during optimization when a minimum or saddle point is encountered. When gradients are zero, the parameters of the neural network do not update, and the network stops learning. This can be problematic, especially if the current solution is not optimal.

NaN Gradients

NaN gradients are usually the result of undefined operations during computation, such as division by zero or taking the log of a negative number. Once a NaN is produced at any point in the computation, it tends to propagate, contaminating the rest of the computation and resulting in an overall result of NaN. In the context of neural network training, if a NaN gradient is encountered, the parameter update is undefined, which can cause the entire training process to fail.

In JAX, you can use the jax.grad function to compute gradients, and it will handle zero and NaN gradients according to the mathematical rules of differentiation. However, it is often beneficial to add checks into your code to handle these cases.

The given below is a simple example that demonstrates handling zero and NaN gradients in JAX:

```python
from jax import grad, jit, value_and_grad
import jax.numpy as jnp
import numpy as np

# define a simple function with a minimum at x=0
def f(x):
    return x ** 2

# compute gradient
dfdx = grad(f)

# compute gradient at minimum
zero_gradient = dfdx(jnp.array(0.0))
print(f"Gradient at minimum (should be 0): {zero_gradient}")

# Now, let us handle a case where NaN gradients might occur

# define a function that has a pole at x=0
def g(x):
    return 1.0 / x

# compute gradient
dgdx = grad(g)

# compute gradient at pole
nan_gradient = dgdx(jnp.array(0.0))
print(f"Gradient at pole (should be NaN): {nan_gradient}")

# To handle this, we could add a small constant to x in the function definition to
# avoid division by zero:
def g_safe(x):
    return 1.0 / (x + 1e-8)
```

```
# compute gradient
dgdx_safe = grad(g_safe)

# compute gradient at pole
safe_gradient = dgdx_safe(jnp.array(0.0))
print(f"Gradient at pole with safe function (should not be NaN): {safe_gradient}")
```

In the above sample program, the function f(x) = x**2 has a minimum at x=0, where the gradient is zero. The function g(x) = 1/x has a pole at x=0, where the gradient is not defined (NaN). In g_safe(x), we add a small constant to x in the denominator to avoid division by zero and get a defined gradient at x=0.

This is a simple example, and the strategies for handling zero and NaN gradients in practice can depend on the specific context. Always remember that understanding your model and the underlying mathematics can help in developing effective strategies for handling such cases.

Summary

In this chapter, we delved into the power of JAX's auto-differentiation capabilities and explored gradients in depth. We began with a basic understanding of automatic differentiation, leveraging computational graphs to compute derivatives. This feature is fundamental in most machine learning algorithms, particularly in training neural networks, where backpropagation is used to adjust the model's weights based on the calculated gradients. A practical example was given to illustrate how JAX simplifies this computation.

The chapter then focused on the computation of Jacobians and Hessians using jax.jacfwd and jax.jacrev functions. These second-order derivatives provide us with more nuanced information about our function, such as curvature, helping us better understand the optimization landscape of our problem. We learned how to utilize these functions in JAX and computed the Jacobian and Hessian matrices of a function using a practical example.

We further delved into nested differentiation for computing higher-order derivatives, a powerful feature in JAX that enables the computation of n-th order derivatives. Lastly, we addressed two special gradient cases: zero and NaN gradients. These cases are critical as they can pose challenges during optimization in machine learning and deep learning models. Strategies were discussed on how to handle such situations, ensuring our models continue learning efficiently and effectively. With JAX's flexible and powerful differentiation capabilities, we are well-equipped to tackle even complex differentiation tasks, paving the way for more sophisticated model design and optimization strategies.

CHAPTER 6: EFFICIENT BATCH PROCESSING WITH JAX

Introducing Vectorization

This chapter delves into the critical field of vectorization, a concept fundamental to numerical computing and machine learning. Vectorization, in its simplest form, refers to the process of executing operations on entire arrays or matrices, instead of conducting them on individual elements. This powerful concept allows for enhanced parallelism, enabling computations to be executed simultaneously, rather than sequentially. This results in considerable performance boosts, as it exploits the inherent capability of modern computing architectures such as CPUs, GPUs, and TPUs to handle large volumes of data in an efficient and streamlined manner.

At the heart of vectorization in JAX is the function known as 'jax.vmap'—the 'vmap' standing for vectorized-map. This transformative function is an integral part of JAX's transformative suite, which includes other powerful functions like grad and jit. The primary purpose of jax.vmap is to facilitate the transformation of functions to operate seamlessly on batch dimensions. Similar in its functionality to a map function, jax.vmap transcends its traditional role by operating in a vectorized manner. In essence, the vectorization function 'maps' an input function over an additional batch dimension. It modifies a function to broadcast over array or batch dimensions, akin to how the np.vectorize() function works in numpy, but with much more efficacy and precision. This capacity for vectorized mapping can pave the way for significant computational speedups, particularly when dealing with high-volume data.

Moreover, the leverage gained by jax.vmap is markedly amplified when combined with hardware accelerators, specifically GPUs and TPUs. These hardware accelerators have been designed and optimized to execute operations on vectors in parallel, thus significantly benefiting from the efficient mapping and vectorization facilitated by jax.vmap. The vmap function, therefore, plays a significant role in parallelizing operations that originally worked on single data points, allowing the operation to handle 'batches' of data points. This operation aligns with the modern hardware design philosophy that advocates parallelism, which is critical for large-scale machine learning tasks.

To sum it up, by providing an efficient and simple method to implement vectorization, JAX's vmap function unlocks powerful computing resources, and lays the groundwork for machine learning professionals to easily scale computations across data batches and perform efficient parallel computation. It's a key tool in the machine learning practitioner's toolbox for harnessing the power of modern hardware and achieving high-performance numerical computation. This exploration into JAX's vectorization capability forms the cornerstone of this chapter, setting the stage for further exploration into the library's features.

Sample Program to Implement Vectorization

Let us illustrate this with a simple example. Consider a function that performs an element-wise operation, like squaring:

```
def square(x):
    return x ** 2
```

We can apply this function to a single number:

```
y = square(2.0)  # output: 4.0
```

Now, if we want to apply this function to a list of numbers (an array), we would traditionally use a Python loop or a list comprehension. However, with jax.vmap, we can do it more efficiently:

```
import jax.numpy as jnp
from jax import vmap

x = jnp.array([1.0, 2.0, 3.0, 4.0])
y = vmap(square)(x)  # output: array([1., 4., 9., 16.])
```

jax.vmap applies the square function to each element of the x array, resulting in a new array y where each element is the square of the corresponding element in x.

In addition to this, JAX also provides another transformation for vectorized operations called jax.lax.scan, which is specifically designed for operations where the output at each position depends on outputs at previous positions (like a cumulative sum). This makes it possible to perform these operations efficiently in parallel on hardware accelerators.

Through its sophisticated set of transformations, JAX provides us with the ability to easily and efficiently vectorize our computations, thereby maximizing performance and efficiency when working with large arrays of data.

Efficient Batch Processing

The use of batch processing is a vital component of both machine learning and deep learning projects, and it is especially important when working with datasets that are both vast and complicated. Using this strategy, rather of carefully processing individual samples one at a time, it is possible to process an entire batch of data in one fell swoop. This method offers a number of benefits, including increased efficiency and a notable reduction in the amount of time required for computational processes. In addition, the full use of hardware parallelism and the functionality of stochastic gradient descent (SGD) and its offshoots are two key reasons that enhance the importance of batch processing.

In this day and age of data-driven applications, hardware accelerators like Graphics Processing Units (GPUs) and Tensor Processing Units (TPUs) have evolved to become an indispensable component of the computing infrastructure. When working with the massive datasets that are typical of applications involving machine learning and deep learning, it is essential to have sophisticated accelerators that are intended specifically for parallel computations. These accelerators have been developed. Because it allows for the processing of several data samples at the same time, batch processing works extremely well in conjunction with these accelerators. Because of this concurrency, one is able to utilize the full capacity of these powerful devices, which results in greatly increased speed and efficiency in operation. By employing batch processing, we can ensure that all of the hardware resources available to us are utilized to their greatest potential, which in turn reduces the amount of time needed for computing and makes our machine learning and deep learning algorithms significantly more efficient.

When it comes to algorithms, batch processing is essential to the operation of optimization techniques such as Stochastic Gradient Descent (SGD) and its numerous variants. When training neural networks, the goal is to have a loss function that is as small as possible. Iteratively updating the model's parameters in the opposite direction of the gradient of the loss function is what is required to accomplish this reduction. Calculating the real gradient, on the other hand, can be a computationally intensive process, particularly for large datasets. At this point, SGD and batch processing become relevant factors. Calculating the gradient for a relatively small batch of samples allows SGD to produce an approximation of the actual gradient while drastically lowering the amount of work required by the algorithm. SGD is able to lower the amount of noise in the gradient estimate by using more than one sample in each batch. This ultimately results in optimization that is more stable and effective. This, in turn, causes a faster convergence of the model to a good solution over the course of time.

In addition, other optimization methods, including mini-batch gradient descent, Adam, and RMSProp, all of which are variants of SGD, depend on batch processing in order to function properly. These techniques also use a batch of data to compute an estimate of the gradient; however, in order to increase efficiency, each of these algorithms adds a unique twist to the standard SGD process. Because these algorithms make use of batches, they are better able to strike a compromise between the precision of the gradient estimate and the computational cost of calculating it, which ultimately leads to more effective learning.

Implementing Batch Processing Efficiently

Let us demonstrate this with the square function from the previous example, now imagining that we need to compute the square of multiple batches of numbers:

```
import jax.numpy as jnp
from jax import vmap

def square(x):
    return x ** 2

# Define a batch of data
x = jnp.array([[1.0, 2.0, 3.0, 4.0],
          [5.0, 6.0, 7.0, 8.0],
          [9.0, 10.0, 11.0, 12.0]])

# We can use vmap to apply the square function to each batch
batch_square = vmap(square)
y = batch_square(x)

print(y)
```

In the above sample program, x is a 2D array, where each row is a batch of numbers. We use vmap to vectorize the square function and apply it to each batch. The result, y, is a new 2D array where each row is the square of the corresponding row in x.

The vmap function automatically detects the batch dimension (by default, it assumes it's the first dimension), and applies the function to each batch. This makes it very efficient for processing large batches of data, as we're able to utilize the parallel processing capabilities of our hardware.

Vmap: Deep Dive

In addition to the basic use we've covered, vmap can also handle functions with multiple inputs and outputs. It will apply the function element-wise to each of the inputs and return corresponding outputs.

For example, consider a function that takes two arrays and returns their element-wise sum and product:

```
def sum_and_product(x, y):
    return x + y, x * y
```

We can use vmap to apply this function to two batches of data:

```
import jax.numpy as jnp
from jax import vmap

# Define two batches of data
x = jnp.array([[1.0, 2.0, 3.0, 4.0],
               [5.0, 6.0, 7.0, 8.0],
               [9.0, 10.0, 11.0, 12.0]])

y = jnp.array([[13.0, 14.0, 15.0, 16.0],
               [17.0, 18.0, 19.0, 20.0],
               [21.0, 22.0, 23.0, 24.0]])

# Use vmap to apply the sum_and_product function to each batch
batch_sum_and_product = vmap(sum_and_product)
sums, products = batch_sum_and_product(x, y)

print("Sums:\n", sums)
print("Products:\n", products)
```

In the above sample program, batch_sum_and_product takes two batches of data, x and y, and returns two batches of results: the element-wise sums and products of x and y.

Further, vmap can also be used with other JAX transformations. For example, you can use vmap and grad together to compute the gradients of a function with respect to a batch of inputs:

```
from jax import grad

def f(x):
    return jnp.sin(x)

# Compute the gradient of f with respect to a batch of inputs
batch_grad_f = vmap(grad(f))
x = jnp.array([0.0, jnp.pi / 2, jnp.pi, 3 * jnp.pi / 2])
grads = batch_grad_f(x)

print("Gradients:\n", grads)
```

In the above sample program, batch_grad_f computes the gradient of the f function (which returns the sine of its input) with respect to each element in a batch of inputs. This makes it easy to compute gradients for a batch of inputs in a single call.

Challenges and Limitations of Vmap

When it comes to deep learning and numerical computing activities, the implementation of vmap in JAX offers a significant amount of flexibility and advantages, particularly in terms of making it easier to do vectorized operations. Nevertheless, it is essential to keep in mind that, just like any other tool or function, vmap has its own restrictions and concerns that need to be properly addressed in order to achieve the highest possible level of performance.

The incompatibility of several procedures with vmap presents itself as one of the first difficulties encountered. For example, certain kinds of indexing or data reshaping might not be easily vectorizable, which would mean that the original function would need to be modified in order to be compatible with vmap. To give you an example, a function that works with integer indices and whose values change depending on the batch dimension could need a significant amount of effort in order to be compatible with jax.vmap. This may require reorganizing or rewriting certain sections of the code, which will add another layer of complexity to the process.

Memory consumption is yet another issue that must be considered when thinking about the use of vmaps. The ability of vmap to support parallel operations can considerably speed up computations. However, in addition to this, they call for the simultaneous storage of intermediate results for each element of the batch, which results in an increased demand on memory. As a consequence of this, the higher memory required may provide substantial issues when working with large batches of data or data that has a high dimension.

Batch size is another factor that can affect how effectively vmap works. Because of its ability to parallelize calculations across the batch dimension, vmap performs exceptionally well when dealing with big batches. However, when dealing with batches of a smaller size, it may be less efficient. In this situation, the overheads that are connected with vmap have the potential to outweigh the benefits that are delivered by parallelization. In these kinds of circumstances, a conventional loop can end up being a more efficient solution.

When working with vmap, one must also take into account the compatibility of their hardware. Even though JAX was developed to run without any problems with modern hardware accelerators like GPUs and TPUs, the speed advantages using vmap could not be as great on CPUs or on some older devices. It's possible that not all hardware or backends fully support or are optimized for vectorized operations, which can lead to performance that is less than ideal.

Another issue that can become more difficult with the use of vmap is debugging. It is possible that debugging code that makes use of vmap will be more difficult than debugging code that makes use of regular Python loops. This is mostly due to the fact that the control flow within the batched calculation will be implicit rather than explicitly given out in the source code. This can make it more difficult to track down problems or defects, which may need more complicated debugging strategies.

When using vmap, the order of operations may be different in the batch computation compared to the original unbatched function. If your function is dependent on side effects or includes operations that are not commutative, this could potentially lead to subtle errors in the function. It is necessary to have an awareness of how the order of operations can change while vectorization is taking place, as well as to carefully design functions that are going to be vectorized using vmap. To summarize, vmap is a strong tool in JAX that enables efficient vectorized operations. However, in order to fully utilize its potential, it is essential to comprehend and navigate its restrictions and concerns. Just as with any other tool, making effective use of vmap necessitates having a comprehensive comprehension of how it operates, meticulous planning, and considerate execution.

Summary

In this chapter, we set out on an adventure to learn about vectorization in JAX and how it improves speed by making use of batch processing. In the beginning, we gained an understanding of the notion of vectorization as well as the part it plays in improving the efficiency of computational processes by performing many data operations simultaneously. This capability to conduct actions on arrays without explicitly looping is especially useful in the context of machine learning, which frequently involves working with enormous data sets.

As we dug deeper into the topic, we were familiar with the powerful JAX transformation known as vmap. This transformation may efficiently apply a function to each individual element of an input array. Through the use of several different instances, we were able to illustrate its capabilities. These examples included the management of functions that had numerous inputs and outputs, as well as the combination of vmap with other JAX transformations, such as grad, for the purpose of computing the gradients of a function with respect to a batch of inputs. We showed how vmap makes fast batch processing possible, as well as its inherent flexibility, which makes it possible for a variety of complex tasks to be created and carried out in an efficient manner.

However, we did exercise caution to ensure that we understood the constraints and potential difficulties associated with utilizing vmap. This includes problems such as higher memory utilization for the storage of intermediate findings, potential inefficiencies with small batch sizes, and obstacles in debugging the program. Additionally, we found that some operations might not be compatible with vmap, which might call for some modifications to the functions involved. In spite of these factors, we discovered that vmap is a flexible tool that, when applied appropriately, has the potential to dramatically accelerate computations in JAX. This is especially true in the fields of machine learning and numerical processing.

CHAPTER 7: POWER OF PARALLEL COMPUTING WITH JAX

Necessity of Parallel Computing in Deep Learning

It has been known for some time that one of the most important success factors in the field of deep learning is the utilization of parallel computing. It is possible to achieve huge increases in training and inference speed by the distribution of computing workloads across numerous processors, which in turn makes it possible to design and deploy models that are both larger and more sophisticated. Up until very recently, practitioners of deep learning depended almost exclusively on manual parallelization approaches or tools supplied by frameworks such as TensorFlow and PyTorch. These tools and approaches, while useful to some degree, frequently demand a large amount of effort as well as an in-depth understanding of the fundamentals of parallel computing. Additionally, they have a propensity to be specialized to a certain hardware configuration, which might result in restricted mobility and scalability.

Consider the process of teaching a large convolutional neural network (CNN) to classify images, for example. When working with huge datasets, training such a model on a single GPU might take a significant amount of time. This is especially true when working with more complex problems. It is common practice to split the computing jobs across numerous GPUs in order to speed up the training process. This helps to speed up the overall process. This could be accomplished by data parallelism, which is the process of breaking the dataset into smaller batches that are then processed in parallel, or by model parallelism, which refers to the process of dividing the model itself across numerous GPUs.

Both of these strategies have the potential to result in a significant increase in speed, but each has its own unique set of obstacles to overcome. Synchronizing and accumulating the gradients computed on each GPU is the fundamental problem when it comes to data parallelism. This can lead to slower convergence or even model divergence if it is not addressed properly. In order to achieve model parallelism, the most important difficulty is to split the model in an effective manner while also handling the communication between the many GPUs. The adjustment of hyperparameters is a typical example of another use case for parallel computing in deep learning. A large number of machine learning algorithms, including deep learning models, call for the selection of appropriate hyperparameters. This, in turn, frequently necessitates training and evaluating the model with a variety of various hyperparameter settings. Because each setting for the hyperparameter can be taught independently, this activity lends itself well to massively parallel processing. The efficient management of these duties and the collection of the outcomes, on the other hand, is not a small matter and requires careful design.

The introduction of Google's JAX library has significantly reduced the complexity of these difficulties. The automatic differentiation and accelerated linear algebra skills that it possesses make the easy implementation of parallel algorithms a reality with this tool. It includes high-level primitives for parallel computation, such as pmap for SPMD style parallelism, which abstracts away many of the complexity required in manual parallelization. This kind of parallelism is known as Single Program, Multiple Data style parallelism. Additionally, it enables smooth switching between different hardware backends, which makes it possible for the same piece of code to execute on CPUs, GPUs, and TPUs with very little to no modification required. This has considerably lowered the barrier to entry for parallel computing in deep learning, making it possible to implement efficient parallel computations with relative ease.

Parallel Computation and pmap

Computing in parallel, or parallel computing, is a powerful aspect of JAX that enables users to make use of several processors to do out computations all at once. It offers two core parallelism primitives: jax.vmap for vectorizing calculations over a batch dimension and jax.pmap for parallelizing computations across leading axes. During this conversation, we'll be concentrating on the jax.pmap file.

For the purpose of expressing single-program, multiple-data (SPMD), computations, the jax.pmap function was developed. In other words, it enables the execution of the same program on multiple processors, each of which may be processing data that is unique to itself. It works in a manner quite similar to that of vmap in that it vectorize a function by mapping it across a leading axis of the inputs that it receives. On the other hand, pmap distributes the processing across numerous devices, such as multiple GPUs or TPUs, rather than vectorizing it on a single device like most other programs do.

To put it simply, the following is how it operates:

jax.pmap is a function that accepts one and applies it to each slice of the input data across all of the devices that are accessible. For instance, if you have 8 GPUs and an input array with a size of 8 along its leading axis, pmap will apply the function to each slice of the array on each GPU independently. This is because each GPU processes the array in its own unique manner. Importantly, pmap takes care of handling the transmission of data across devices on its own.

Consider the following code snippet as an example:

```
from jax import random, pmap
import jax.numpy as jnp
```

```
key = random.PRNGKey(0)
keys = random.split(key, 8)

# Assuming you have 8 devices
padded_pmap = pmap(lambda key: random.normal(key, (5000,)),
devices=jax.devices()[:8])
padded_pmap(keys)
```

In the above sample program, pmap generates normal random numbers in parallel across 8 devices. Each device generates a tensor of shape (5000,) independently.

Although it may appear to be simple, it is essential to have an understanding of some of the nuances and restrictions involved. An additional leading dimension, referred to as the batch dimension, must be included in the input to pmap. This dimension must correspond to the number of devices among which the computation is distributed. This indicates that you will need to organize your data in such a way that it is possible for the computation to be correctly partitioned across devices. Also, while pmap handles data transfer between devices, data transfer can be expensive and may eat into the speedup gained through parallelization if it is not controlled correctly. This can be avoided, however, by carefully managing data transfer. When utilized in conjunction with other JAX features like as jit, grad, and vmap, the full potential of pmap's capabilities is brought to light. Because of this, it is possible to carry out complicated computations in parallel while simultaneously optimizing performance and carrying out automatic differentiation.

It is important to point out that JAX was developed with the principle in mind that the explicit location of your device should be the exception, rather than the rule. This is mostly as a result of the fact that explicit device placement can sometimes result in code that is less portable. As a result, the majority of the time, JAX's default device assignment ought to be sufficient.

Efficient Parallel Computing Strategies

Parallel computing strategies in JAX can significantly speed up your machine learning and deep learning experiments. Below are a few strategies to consider:

Data Parallelism

This strategy involves dividing your data into smaller batches and processing each batch on a different device simultaneously. JAX provides the pmap function to make data parallelism straightforward.

Let us consider we have a simple function to calculate the square of a number. In a data-parallel scenario, we can calculate the square of multiple numbers across multiple devices. Below is an example:

```
from jax import pmap
import jax.numpy as jnp


# Assume you have 8 devices
@pmap
def square(x):
    return x ** 2

inputs = jnp.arange(8)  # [0, 1, 2, 3, 4, 5, 6, 7]
outputs = square(inputs)
```

In the above sample program, each element in the input array is squared on a separate device.

Model Parallelism

This strategy involves splitting your model across multiple devices. This is particularly useful when your model is too large to fit on a single device. However, implementing model parallelism manually can be complex. JAX simplifies this through sharded_jit, which allows you to specify how different parts of your computation should be placed on different devices.

Below is a simplified example of model parallelism:

```
from jax.experimental.maps import mesh
import jax.numpy as jnp
from jax import random, pmap
```

```
from flax.linen import Dense, nn

def model_parallel(rng, inputs):
    layer1 = Dense(features=1000)
    layer2 = Dense(features=1000)
    layer3 = Dense(features=10)

    with mesh(jax.devices(), ('devices',)):
        h = layer1(inputs)
        h = pmap(layer2)(h)
        h = pmap(layer3)(h)
    return h

rng = random.PRNGKey(0)
inputs = jnp.ones((8, 1000))
model_parallel(rng, inputs)
```

In the above sample program, Dense layers are split across multiple devices, with each device handling a different part of the computation.

Combining Data and Model Parallelism

In many cases, the most efficient way to parallelize your computation is to combine data parallelism and model parallelism. This can be achieved in JAX using a combination of pmap and sharded_jit.

Below is a simple example:

```
def combined_parallelism(rng, inputs):
    layer1 = Dense(features=1000)
    layer2 = Dense(features=1000)
    layer3 = Dense(features=10)

    with mesh(jax.devices(), ('devices',)):
        h = pmap(layer1)(inputs)
```

```
    h = pmap(layer2)(h)
    h = pmap(layer3)(h)
  return h

rng = random.PRNGKey(0)
inputs = jnp.ones((8, 1000))
combined_parallelism(rng, inputs)
```

This example combines data and model parallelism by using pmap to process different batches of data on different devices, while also splitting the computation of each layer across multiple devices.

Communication Strategies

In a parallel computing environment, different devices often need to communicate with each other, e.g., to aggregate gradients during backpropagation. JAX provides several primitives for inter-device communication, such as jax.lax.psum for summing values across devices, jax.lax.ppermute for arbitrary permutation of data across devices, and jax.lax.pshuffle for collective permutation of data across devices. By carefully choosing and using these communication primitives, you can greatly optimize the performance of your parallel computations.

To sum it up, parallel computing in JAX involves a combination of strategies and techniques, including data and model parallelism, judicious use of parallelism primitives, and efficient inter-device communication. By mastering these strategies, you can write highly efficient and scalable machine learning and deep learning code using JAX.

Pmap for Training Neural Networks across Multiple Devices

In this section, we will see how pmap can be used for training a simple neural network across multiple devices in parallel. For this demonstration, let us consider a simple fully connected neural network with two hidden layers. We'll use the MNIST dataset for simplicity.

The steps are as follows:

Prepare the Dataset

We first load and prepare the dataset. The MNIST dataset is commonly used in machine learning and is readily available in many libraries. For simplicity, we will use the one available in TensorFlow datasets.

```
import tensorflow_datasets as tfds

# Load the MNIST dataset
mnist_dataset, mnist_info = tfds.load(name="mnist", with_info=True,
as_supervised=True)

# Split the data into train and test
mnist_train, mnist_test = mnist_dataset['train'], mnist_dataset['test']
```

Preprocessing

For simplicity, we will scale the images to [0, 1] and flatten them into vectors.

```
def preprocess(sample):
    image, label = sample
    image = tf.image.convert_image_dtype(image, tf.float32).numpy()
    image = image.flatten()
    return image, label
mnist_train = map(preprocess, mnist_train)
mnist_test = map(preprocess, mnist_test)
```

Define the Model

Let us create a simple fully connected network with two hidden layers.

```
from flax.linen import Module, Dense, relu
import jax.numpy as jnp

class MLP(Module):
```

```python
def setup(self):
    self.layer1 = Dense(features=128)
    self.layer2 = Dense(features=64)
    self.layer3 = Dense(features=10)

def __call__(self, x):
    x = relu(self.layer1(x))
    x = relu(self.layer2(x))
    x = self.layer3(x)
    return x

# Instantiate the model
model = MLP()
```

Define the Loss Function and Optimizer

Let us use the cross-entropy loss and a simple SGD optimizer.

```python
from jax import grad, jit
from flax.optim import GradientDescent
from flax.linen import ParamState
from flax import optim
from jax.nn import softmax_cross_entropy

# Define the loss function
def loss_fn(params, inputs, targets):
    logits = model.apply(params, inputs)
    loss = softmax_cross_entropy(logits, targets).mean()
    return loss

# Define the optimizer
optimizer = GradientDescent(learning_rate=0.01)
```

Parallelize Training Loop using pmap

Finally, we can use pmap to parallelize the training across multiple devices. This is where the power of JAX really shines.

```
from jax import pmap, random
import numpy as np

# Initialize parameters
params = model.init(ParamState(), random.PRNGKey(0), jnp.ones([1, 784]))

# Wrap the loss function and the update function with pmap
@pmap
def pmapped_loss_fn(params, inputs, targets):
    return loss_fn(params, inputs, targets)

@pmap
def pmapped_update(params, inputs, targets):
    grads = grad(pmapped_loss_fn)(params, inputs, targets)
    params = optimizer.apply_gradient(params, grads)
    return params

# Train the model
for epoch in range(10):
    for batch in mnist_train:
        inputs, targets = batch
        # Ensure the data is evenly divisible across devices
        inputs = np.repeat(inputs, num_devices, axis=0)
        targets = np.repeat(targets, num_devices, axis=0)
        params = pmapped_update(params, inputs, targets)
```

In the above sample program, pmap is used to automatically parallelize the computation of gradients and the application of these gradients to update the model's parameters. Note that the use of pmap requires that the data be evenly divisible across devices (which we ensure by using np.repeat), and that each device has the same copy of the parameters and gets a different slice of the input data.

This example demonstrates how to leverage the power of JAX's pmap function for efficient parallel computation in machine learning and deep learning applications.

Using pmap for Collective Operations

Let us illustrate how JAX's pmap function can be used for collective operations in distributed computing. Collective operations are those operations that involve communication between multiple devices, such as summing values across devices or broadcasting a value from one device to all other devices.

We'll walk through an example where we distribute data across multiple devices, perform a computation on each device, and then sum the results across all devices.

```
from jax import pmap, lax, random
import jax.numpy as jnp

# Assume we have 8 devices
num_devices = 8

# Create some data for each device
keys = random.split(random.PRNGKey(0), num_devices)

# Define a function to perform on each device
def square_and_sum(key):
    # Each device gets different random data
    data = random.normal(key, (5000, 5000))
    return jnp.sum(data ** 2)

# Now let us map this function across all devices
result = pmap(square_and_sum)(keys)

# At this point, `result` is an array of shape (num_devices,) with the sum of
```

squares
computed on each device. To get the total sum across all devices, we can use `pmap` again
with the `lax.psum` function, which performs a sum across all devices:

```
total_result = pmap(lax.psum)(result).get()[0]
```

In the above sample program, we start by generating different random keys for each device. Then we define a function, square_and_sum, which generates some random data (different for each device, thanks to the different keys), squares it, and sums it up.

We use pmap to map this function across all devices. At this point, we have an array with the sum of squares computed on each device. To get the total sum across all devices, we use pmap again, but this time with the lax.psum function, which performs a sum across all devices. This is an example of a collective operation, as it involves communication between the devices. In the end, we call .get()[0] on the result to get the total sum as a scalar value. This example demonstrates the power of JAX's pmap function for performing distributed computations and collective operations across multiple devices, providing a simple and efficient way to perform large-scale computations.

Summary

In this chapter, we went deeper into the idea of parallel computing and its usefulness in deep learning. In particular, we focused on how JAX has made parallel computing more accessible and efficient. We talked about the difficulties that were there in the field of parallel computing before the development of JAX. These difficulties included the intricacies of designing parallel programs and coordinating memory across several devices. This paved the way for us to investigate the pmap function of the JAX programming language, which is a potent instrument that facilitates parallelization and handles these issues automatically.

Following that, we delved headfirst into the inner workings of pmap, dissecting its operation and analyzing how well it deals with parallel calculations. In addition to this, we emphasized the significance of other methods for achieving effective parallelization, such as data parallelism, model parallelism, and pipelining. Pipelining is the process of arranging activities in such a way as to minimize idle time on any device. Data parallelism refers to the practice of dividing a dataset into several devices, while model parallelism refers to the practice of dividing a model's layers or parameters among numerous devices. In order to better comprehend how each of these tactics should be implemented, we provided specific examples to illustrate each one.

In the last part of this lesson, we covered the practical implementation of pmap in a deep learning project. We began with the distribution of simple data across multiple devices and progressed all the way up to the performance of parallel computations and collective operations. With the assistance of pmap and lax.psum, we were able to describe collective operations, which are operations that involve communication between several devices and include activities such as summing values or broadcasting values. At the end of the chapter, we came away with an in-depth comprehension of how JAX enables powerful, efficient, and easy parallel computing in applications that involve deep learning. The hands-on examples should equip you to start exploiting JAX's pmap in your own applications by providing you with the necessary tools.

CHAPTER 8: TRAINING NEURAL NETWORKS WITH JAX

Potential of JAX in Training Deep Learning

Within the realms of machine learning and deep learning, JAX plays an essential and multifaceted role in research and development. JAX is an essential component in the study of self-supervised learning, which is quickly gaining traction as a potentially fruitful subfield within deep learning. Learning through self-supervision makes use of unlabeled input in order to acquire usable representations. This method, which is frequently utilized with huge neural networks, is computationally costly and necessitates the flexibility and performance that are offered by JAX. Researchers and engineers may swiftly cycle over a variety of learning methods and architectures with the help of JAX. This enables them to optimize their code for performance and make good use of the hardware resources that are readily available. In addition, because JAX integrates so readily with well-known deep learning libraries like TensorFlow and PyTorch, it is simple to modify already-running projects so that they may make use of the capabilities provided by JAX. Because of this, it is an extremely useful instrument in production settings, which place a premium on speed, efficiency, and adaptability. JAX allows programmers to build high-performance code for machine learning that is also simple to comprehend, bug test, and maintain in their applications.

Training deep learning models is a difficult process that requires a significant investment of time and resources, particularly when working with huge datasets. When it comes to training in a quick and efficient manner, having the ability to effectively harness the power of GPUs and TPUs is crucial. In this context, the capability of JAX to divide computations over several devices while also managing memory is of tremendous benefit. In addition, the functional programming style that JAX employs makes it easier to write code that is both simple and short, even when applied to complicated machine learning algorithms. Last but not least, JAX's capabilities go well beyond only model training. Because of its impressive numerical computing capabilities, it is well suited for additional machine learning tasks, including data pretreatment, feature extraction, and model evaluation. For instance, the process of preparing data for machine learning models may be made much simpler and carried out at a much faster pace thanks to the superior indexing and efficient batch processing capabilities offered by JAX. JAX offers solutions to a significant number of the difficulties and complications that are associated with deep learning. It is compatible with several of the most prominent deep learning libraries, in addition to its ability to conduct fast numerical computing, autodifferentiation, and parallel calculations. These capabilities, along with its compatibility with these libraries, make it an invaluable tool for deep learning specialists.

Training RNN Model for Sentiment Analysis

Consider the following illustration of a straightforward Recurrent Neural Network for the purpose of doing sentiment analysis. The purpose of the network is to determine if a sentence is optimistic or pessimistic based on the order in which the words appear in the sentence. The word order in the sentence will serve as the input, and the evaluation of the statement's tone, expressed as positive or negative, will be the output.

To begin, let us import any necessary libraries and configure our random number generator by setting the seed:

```
import jax
import jax.numpy as jnp
from jax import random, grad, jit, vmap
from flax import linen as nn


# Set the seed for reproducibility
key = random.PRNGKey(0)
```

Now, let us define our RNN. We will use the flax.linen module for this, which is a high-level neural network library that works well with JAX:

```
class RNN(nn.Module):
    num_classes: int  # number of output classes
    hidden_dim: int  # hidden dimension of RNN

    def setup(self):
        self.rnn_cell = nn.rnn_cell.BasicRNNCell(name="rnn_cell")
        self.dense_layer = nn.Dense(self.num_classes,
kernel_init=nn.initializers.xavier_uniform(), name="dense")

    def __call__(self, inputs):
        seq_len, batch_size, _ = inputs.shape
        hidden_state = self.rnn_cell.initialize_carry(jax.random.PRNGKey(0),
(batch_size,), self.hidden_dim)
```

```
    for t in range(seq_len):
        hidden_state, _ = self.rnn_cell(hidden_state, inputs[t])

    output = self.dense_layer(hidden_state)
    return output
```

We will also define a loss function that we will try to minimize during training:

```
def cross_entropy_loss(logits, labels):
    return -jnp.mean(jnp.log(nn.softmax(logits))[jnp.arange(labels.shape[0]), labels])
```

Next, we will define our update function. This function will be used to update the weights of our network based on the gradients computed:

```
@jax.jit
def update(params, inputs, targets, lr=0.1):
    # Compute the gradients of the loss with respect to the parameters
    grads = jax.grad(cross_entropy_loss)(params, inputs, targets)

    # Update the parameters by subtracting the gradients times the learning rate
    new_params = jax.tree_multimap(lambda p, g: p - lr * g, params, grads)
    return new_params
```

Now, we can start the training process. First, we will initialize our model and the parameters:

```
# Initialize the model
model = RNN(num_classes=2, hidden_dim=64)
params = model.init(jax.random.PRNGKey(0), jnp.ones((10, 1, 100)))  # assuming
input shape is (seq_len, batch_size, input_dim)

# Training loop
```

```
for epoch in range(num_epochs):
    for inputs, targets in data:  # replace 'data' with your actual data
        params = update(params, inputs, targets)
```

The above is a straightforward illustration of how to train an RNN utilizing JAX. In actual reality, you would also want to integrate a validation loop to track the performance of the model during training on a different validation set, and you might implement early stopping or model checkpointing to save the model that performs the best overall. It is important that you take into consideration the fact that this piece of code presupposes that you already own your data in the form of sequence inputs and associated targets. In order to complete this form, you will need to prepare your actual data.

Training CNN Model for Image Classification

As an illustration, we will utilize a straightforward convolutional neural network (CNN) to perform an image classification task. We will employ a straightforward architecture that consists of two convolutional layers followed by one fully linked layer. The images themselves will serve as the input, and the resulting output will be a classification scheme for the many categories that these pictures fall into.

To begin, we will import the necessary modules, which are as follows:

```
import jax
import jax.numpy as jnp
from jax import random, grad, jit, vmap
from flax import linen as nn

# Set the seed for reproducibility
key = random.PRNGKey(0)
```

Let us define our CNN:

```
class CNN(nn.Module):
    num_classes: int  # number of output classes
```

```python
def setup(self):
    self.conv_layer1 = nn.Conv(features=32, kernel_size=(5, 5))
    self.conv_layer2 = nn.Conv(features=64, kernel_size=(5, 5))
    self.dense_layer = nn.Dense(self.num_classes)

def __call__(self, inputs):
    x = nn.relu(self.conv_layer1(inputs))
    x = nn.max_pool(x, window_shape=(2, 2), strides=(2, 2))
    x = nn.relu(self.conv_layer2(x))
    x = nn.max_pool(x, window_shape=(2, 2), strides=(2, 2))
    x = x.reshape((x.shape[0], -1))  # flatten
    x = self.dense_layer(x)
    return x
```

The loss function we use is the cross entropy loss:

```python
def cross_entropy_loss(logits, labels):
    return -jnp.mean(jnp.log(nn.softmax(logits))[jnp.arange(labels.shape[0]), labels])
```

We then define our update function. This function is used to update the weights of our network based on the gradients:

```python
@jax.jit
def update(params, inputs, targets, lr=0.1):
    grads = jax.grad(cross_entropy_loss)(params, inputs, targets)
    new_params = jax.tree_multimap(lambda p, g: p - lr * g, params, grads)
    return new_params
```

And now, we are ready to train our model. First, we initialize our model and the parameters:

```python
# Initialize the model
model = CNN(num_classes=10)
```

```
params = model.init(jax.random.PRNGKey(0), jnp.ones((1, 28, 28, 1)))  #
assuming input shape is (batch_size, height, width, channels)

# Training loop
for epoch in range(num_epochs):
    for inputs, targets in data:  # replace 'data' with your actual data
        params = update(params, inputs, targets)
```

This is a very good demonstration of how to train a CNN by using JAX. Throughout any CNN model, you will first need to organize your data so that it takes the form of photographs and the classes that correlate to those images. You have the option of preprocessing your data in order to fulfill the prerequisites for the model's input, which in this instance is a four-dimensional tensor with dimensions that correspond, in this order, to the batch size, picture height, image width, and number of channels.

Using JAX for Bayesian Regression

Let us design a Bayesian linear regression model with the form $y = X * w + b$, where the purpose is to learn the weights w and bias b from the data X, y. The model will have the form $y = X * w + b$. In a Bayesian framework, rather than looking for a single optimal set of parameters, the goal is to find a distribution over all of the potential parameter values.

To begin, let us begin by importing the required libraries.

```
import jax.numpy as jnp
import numpy as np
from jax import random, vmap
import matplotlib.pyplot as plt
from numpyro import handlers
import numpyro.distributions as dist
from numpyro.infer import MCMC, NUTS
import numpyro
```

Now, we'll simulate some data to fit our model.

```
np.random.seed(0)  # for reproducibility
n = 100  # number of data points
X = np.random.normal(size=(n, 1))
w_true = np.array([[3.]])
b_true = np.array([2.])
noise = np.random.normal(scale=0.5, size=(n, 1))
y = np.dot(X, w_true) + b_true + noise
```

Next, we'll define our model.

```
def model(X, y):
    w = numpyro.sample('w', dist.Normal(jnp.zeros(X.shape[1]),
jnp.ones(X.shape[1])))
    b = numpyro.sample('b', dist.Normal(0., 10.))
    sigma = numpyro.sample('sigma', dist.HalfCauchy(1.))
    mu = jnp.dot(X, w) + b
    numpyro.sample('y', dist.Normal(mu, sigma), obs=y)
```

The model defines a Normal prior over w and b, and a HalfCauchy prior over sigma (the noise standard deviation). mu is the mean of the likelihood, and is a deterministic function of the inputs X, the weights w, and the bias b. The model specifies a Normal likelihood with this mean and noise level sigma.

Next, let us use the No-U-Turn Sampler (NUTS) to draw samples from the posterior given this model and data.

```
nuts_kernel = NUTS(model)
mcmc = MCMC(nuts_kernel, num_warmup=500, num_samples=1000)
rng_key = random.PRNGKey(0)
mcmc.run(rng_key, X, y)
```

Once the MCMC algorithm is finished, we can look at the posterior distributions of the parameters.

mcmc.print_summary()

We can also extract the samples to perform any additional analysis or create predictive models.

samples = mcmc.get_samples()

Finally, let us create a predictive model.

predictive = handlers.seed(handlers.condition(model, samples),
rng_seed=rng_key)
vmap_args = (random.split(rng_key, n), X)
predictions = vmap(lambda rng, x: predictive(x, None))(vmap_args)

You now have a predictive Bayesian linear regression model with JAX and NumPyro.

Using JAX for Performance Tuning

Exploiting JAX's characteristics to make efficient use of hardware resources, primarily through vectorization and parallelization, is a significant part of performance tuning in JAX and deep learning. This is true especially for the former.

There are many other approaches one can take, including the following:

JIT Compilation

Always JIT compile your functions whenever possible to optimize execution time. The JIT compiler translates Python code into highly optimized machine code, reducing overhead and enhancing speed.

```
@jax.jit
def function_name(args):
    # function code
```

Just remember not to put code inside jit that you want to be executed every time (like print statements), as jit will compile the function once and then use that compiled version.

Vectorization with vmap

Instead of processing data one at a time, process it in batches using vmap. This can drastically improve performance as modern CPUs and GPUs are designed to perform the same operation on large amounts of data simultaneously. You can use the RNN and CNN training examples from previous chapters or sections, and use vmap to vectorize the batch operations.

Use pmap for Multi-Core Parallelization

If you're working on multiple cores or multiple devices, you can use pmap to parallelize the computation across those cores or devices. This is especially useful when you're training models on large scale distributed systems.

Use Preferred Memory Copying Commands

In JAX, use device_put function to transfer data between host (CPU) and device (GPU/TPU) which is much faster and optimized compared to basic array copying using jnp.array.

Use of Float32 over Float64

Float32 computations are faster and are the default on GPUs. It's often beneficial to use Float32 over Float64 for deep learning applications. However, be cautious of numerical precision issues.

Efficiently use PRNGs

JAX's random functions can create multiple random numbers simultaneously. This is more efficient than creating them one at a time in a loop.

```
rng = jax.random.PRNGKey(0)
numbers = jax.random.normal(rng, shape=(10,))
```

Control Flow Optimizations

If your code involves control flows (like conditionals or loops), consider rewriting them in terms of JAX's control flow operations (jax.lax.cond, jax.lax.scan, jax.lax.while_loop etc.), as these are designed to work efficiently with JAX's JIT compiler.

To sum it up, tuning JAX for performance involves using the primitives provided by the library to best exploit hardware parallelism, reduce Python overhead, and optimize memory use. It's a process of understanding the nuances of JAX and applying that understanding to your specific machine learning or deep learning application.

Summary

This chapter focuses on the multifaceted function that JAX plays in the fields of deep learning and machine learning, as well as the ways in which it accelerates and improves the accuracy of numerical computations, in particular those that arise during the process of model training. It emphasized the manner in which JAX solves the obstacles provided in standard Python libraries and frameworks, particularly when it comes to using current hardware architectures such as GPUs and TPUs.

We proceeded with our exploration of practical applications by talking about the process of training RNN, CNN, and Bayesian models with JAX. We investigated the use of JAX functions in the construction of these models, as well as the powerful role that auto-differentiation plays in making the process of training these models more straightforward. Each of these real-world applications served as a demonstration of the incorporation of JAX into real-world applications, highlighting the power of JAX to improve the efficiency of numerical computations and reduce the amount of time required for training.

The chapter came to a close with a comprehensive conversation regarding performance tuning options in JAX. It emphasized how to maximize the efficiency of JAX by utilizing JIT compilation, vectorization through the use of vmap, multi-core parallelization through the use of pmap, and effective use of preferred memory copying instructions and PRNGs. In addition to that, it recommended using Float32 rather than Float64 for speed improvements and control flow modifications in order to make calculation more efficient. These tactics for performance optimization provide vital insights into fully using the capabilities of JAX in deep learning applications, which makes it a go-to library for activities that are performance-critical.

Thank You

Index

X

Z

Epilogue

As we reach the end of our journey through this book, I hope you have gained a rich understanding of JAX, its potential and advantages over other traditional libraries. We've dived into the depth of JAX, not just in theory but also in practical terms, looking at code examples and running deep learning experiments, truly comprehending its power and flexibility.

Our exploration began with the basics, understanding the importance and need for JAX in numerical computing and how it surpasses the limitations posed by traditional libraries. We meticulously examined its installation across different hardware platforms such as CPU, GPU and TPU, ensuring that you can leverage the most out of your hardware with JAX. The middle chapters of the book walked you through the advanced numerical operations of JAX, with a special focus on JIT compilation, automatic differentiation, vectorization, and parallel computing. In addition to understanding these concepts theoretically, you learned to apply them practically in a coding context, equipping you with an invaluable skill set.

The later part of the book was all about applying JAX in real-world machine learning and deep learning tasks, dealing with complex architectures such as RNNs, CNNs and Bayesian models. You've learned not only to implement these models but also to optimize their performance with the advanced features provided by JAX. In the final chapters, we ventured into the advanced features of JAX that make it a perfect fit for production-grade applications. We talked about the different parallel computing strategies and how to efficiently use JAX's 'pmap' function for distributed computing. We even touched on performance tuning strategies that can further elevate the speed and efficiency of your deep learning models.

As you finish reading this book, I hope you feel empowered to leverage JAX in your upcoming projects, be it machine learning or deep learning. Remember, the ultimate goal of this book was not just to teach you about JAX, but to enable you to harness its full potential, providing an edge in your future endeavors.

JAX is a rapidly evolving library, and while we've covered a lot in this book, there's always more to learn and explore. I encourage you to keep experimenting, keep learning and always stay up-to-date with the latest developments in this exciting field. Finally, I'd like to express my gratitude for joining me on this journey of exploring JAX. It has been a pleasure to guide you through this dynamic and exciting library. Here's to your future success in machine learning and deep learning experiments using JAX!